F o u r t

THE
NEW JERSEY
NOTARY LAW
PRIMER

*All the hard-to-find information
every New Jersey Notary Public
needs to know!*

National Notary Association

For the latest updates on state laws
and requirements, please visit

NationalNotary.org/Primer-Updates

Published by
National Notary Association
9350 De Soto Ave.
Chatsworth, CA 91311-4926
(818) 739-4000
Fax: (818) 700-0920
Website: www.NationalNotary.org
Email: nna@nationalnotary.org

The information in this *Primer* is correct and current at the time
of its publication, although new laws, regulations and rulings may
subsequently affect the validity of certain sections. This information
is provided to aid comprehension of state Notary Public requirements
and should not be construed as legal advice. Please consult an
attorney for inquiries relating to legal matters.

Fourth Edition, Fourth Printing
First Edition © 1994

ISBN 1-59767-000-6

Table
of Contents

Introduction

You are to be commended on your interest in New Jersey Notary law! Purchasing *The New Jersey Notary Law Primer* identifies you as a conscientious professional who takes your official responsibilities seriously.

In few fields is the expression "more to it than meets the eye" truer than in Notary law. What often appears on the surface to be a simple procedure may, in fact, have important legal considerations.

The purpose of *The New Jersey Notary Law Primer* is to provide you with a resource to help decipher the many intricate laws that affect notarization. In doing so, the *Primer* will acquaint you with all important aspects of New Jersey's Notary law and with prudent notarial practices in general.

This edition of *The New Jersey Notary Law Primer* has been updated to include all of the pertinent law changes, including increases in the fees Notaries may charge that became effective in 2002.

While *The New Jersey Notary Law Primer* begins with informative chapters on how to obtain your commission, what tools the Notary needs, often-asked questions, and critical steps in notarization, the heart of this book is the chapter entitled "Notary Laws Explained." Here, we take you through the myriad of Notary laws and put them in easy-to-understand terms. Every section of the law is analyzed and explained, as well as topics not covered by New Jersey law but nonetheless of vital concern to you as a Notary.

For handy reference, we have reprinted the complete text of the laws of New Jersey that relate to Notaries Public. In addition, we have included addresses and phone numbers of Department of Treasury offices, County Clerk offices and Bureaus of Vital Statistics, plus a list of nations that are parties to the Hague Convention, a treaty which simplifies the process of authentication.

Whether you're about to be commissioned for the first time, or are a longtime Notary, we're sure *The New Jersey Notary Law Primer* will provide you with new insight and understanding. Your improved comprehension of New Jersey's Notary law will naturally result in your greater competence as a professional Notary Public.

Milton G. Valera
President
National Notary Association

How to Become a New Jersey Notary Public

1. Ensure that you comply with the basic qualifications for a New Jersey Notary commission.

You must meet the basic requirements to become a Notary in the state of New Jersey. First, you must be 18 years of age or older. Second, you must be a New Jersey resident or a resident of an adjoining state who maintains a business or office in the state. And third, you must not have been convicted of a crime involving dishonesty or a crime in the first or second degree.

Though not stipulated in New Jersey law, an applicant should also be able to read, write and understand the English language.

U.S. citizenship is not required as long as you legally reside in this country under federal law. There is no minimum time of state residency — you can apply for a commission on the same day you enter New Jersey.

2. Obtain a commission application and Notary informational materials.

Both new and renewing Notaries must obtain a commission application from the local county clerk or the State Treasurer. An application may be sent to the State Treasurer at: State of New Jersey, Division of Revenue, Notary Public Section, P.O. Box 452, Trenton, New Jersey 08625. Applications are also available by calling the Notary Public Section at (609) 292-9292, or from the Internet on the home page of the Division of Commercial Recording at:
http://www.state.nj.us/treasury/revenue/dcr/geninfo/corpman.html.

Should you choose to receive the application from the county clerk, a list of county clerk offices is provided on pages 104–105. Although applications are available from any of the county clerk offices, applicants may choose to contact the county clerk's office located in the county where the applicant resides or is employed.

For Notary applicants seeking to renew their commissions, the State Treasurer will usually send a renewal application to Notaries approximately three months prior to the expiration date of the current commission. However, it is important to note that this service is reliable only if the Notary's address on record is current; the Notary is ultimately responsible for obtaining the application for commission renewal.

3. Study the New Jersey Notary Public laws.

Along with the commission application, you will also receive a summary of the pertinent New Jersey laws regarding Notaries. Although New Jersey does not require prospective Notaries to pass an exam, they should study the laws thoroughly to become familiar with notarial acts and duties.

It is also helpful to review the "Notary Laws Explained" chapter of this *Primer*, starting on page 21. The applicable New Jersey statutes are reprinted in the back of this *Primer*, beginning on page 81.

4. Complete the application.

Follow the instructions on the application and complete the application in blue or black ink. You may not use a post office box as an address on the application. In addition, a married woman must use her own name, not that of her spouse (for example, "Jane Smith," not "Mrs. John Smith"). Sign and date the form, using the exact signature you will affix when signing notarial certificates.

Be aware that any false statements or omission of any information required by the application is cause for denial of a Notary commission. In addition, the State Treasurer may reject an application for an applicant's conviction in New Jersey or any other state or U.S. jurisdiction of a crime involving dishonesty (e.g., forgery, counterfeiting) or of certain crimes in the first or second degree.

Before being submitted to the Department of Treasury's Notary Public Section, the completed application form must be endorsed by a member of the New Jersey Legislature, the Secretary of State or the Assistant Secretary of State. (If you do not know who your local legislator is or how to contact him or her, call the Notary Public Section at (609) 292-9292 for more information.)

Mail the completed and endorsed form with a $25 check or money order (payable to the Department of Treasury) to: Notary Public Section, P.O. Box 452, Trenton, NJ 08625.

Nonresident Notary-applicants who reside in an adjoining state and are employed in New Jersey must file an affidavit with the State Treasurer. The affidavit must include the applicant's residence address in the adjoining state and the applicant's place of business in New Jersey. It should be submitted with the application form to the Notary Public Section, P.O. Box 452, Trenton, NJ 08625.

5. Wait for your commission to be returned to you by the Notary Public Section.

The Notary Public Section will review the application form for completeness, endorsement, qualifications and fee. If accepted, the applicant will receive a Notary Public Commission Certificate and an Oath Qualification Certificate.

If rejected, the applicant will receive the application with a rejection notice asking for additional information and resubmission, if appropriate.

6. Take the commission and qualification certificates to the county clerk.

Once the application has been accepted and the applicant has received the Notary Public Commission Certificate and the Oath Qualification Certificate from the Notary Public Section, the applicant must take the certificates to the county clerk in the county in which the applicant resides.

In the case of nonresident applicants, the applicant should take the Commission Certificate and the Oath Qualification Certificate to the county clerk of the county in which the applicant is employed or maintains a business.

Failure to file with the county clerk within three months after the date listed on the Commission Certificate will invalidate the commission and result in forfeiture of the $25 application fee.

7. Take your oath.

The county clerk will administer an oath or affirmation to the applicant. The applicant must present the Oath Qualification Certificate before an oath will be administered.

The county clerk will collect oath, administration and filing fees according to that particular county's fee schedule. (This fee differs for each county. The applicant should contact the specific county in which he or she is filing to determine the applicable fee.)

The county clerk will then return the Oath Qualification Certificate to the Notary Public Section, thereby completing the application process. The Notary is now ready to begin notarizing.■

Tools of the Trade

There are several tools that Notaries need to carry out their duties lawfully and efficiently. These tools are as important to the Notary as a hammer and saw are to the carpenter.

Inking Seal

Although not required by New Jersey law, many of the state's Notaries elect to use an inking stamp to impart an appropriate sense of ceremony to their official acts.

An inking seal allows the Notary to comply with the New Jersey statute (NJSA 52:7-19) requiring the Notary's name to be printed, typed or stamped on every document notarized. The Notary Public manual also requires that the Notary's commission expiration date be stamped, printed or typed on each notarization.

Seal Embosser

While not required by New Jersey law, the seal embosser is used in many states and is often vital on documents sent abroad. Many New Jersey Notaries opt to affix an embossment in addition to an inked seal (if used) impression.

The seal embosser makes a nonphotographically reproducible indentation on the document. Because photocopies of documents can easily pass as originals, the embossment can be used to distinguish an original from a photocopy. Also, embossing all pages in a document together can safeguard against later substitution or addition of pages.

Journal of Notarial Acts

Though New Jersey law does not expressly require Notaries to keep a journal, New Jersey statute does stipulate that each Notary must take an oath of office swearing that he or she will keep a true and accurate record of all notarial acts. In addition, Notaries who execute protests are required to maintain a record of such acts.

The Notary's journal provides a chronological record of notarial transactions that may be used as evidence in a court proceeding and is the best protection for a Notary against claims of misconduct or negligence.

Bound Notary journals with numbered pages have proven to be the safest and most fraud-resistant type of record book. By contrast, loose-leaf books are the least secure. (See "Journal of Notarial Acts," pages 48-50.)

Jurat Stamp

The jurat stamp impresses on an affidavit or other document the jurat wording, "Subscribed and sworn to before me this _____ day of _____, _____ by _____." The jurat stamp is more convenient (and safer, since critical wording will not be omitted) than typing the wording on each document that requires it.

Venue Stamp

The venue stamp is most commonly used in conjunction with the jurat stamp. The phrase, "State of _____, County of _____," indicates where the jurat was executed. The venue stamp may also be used on acknowledgments.

Fingerprinting Device

Though not required by law, asking a signer to leave a thumbprint in the Notary's journal is a strong deterrent to fraud. Small, inexpensive devices make taking a print easy.

Notarial Certificates

Convenient, preprinted notarial certificates for jurats, acknowledgments, proofs of execution by a subscribing witness and for copy certification by a document custodian are available. (See "Notarial Certificates," pages 50-54)

Errors and Omissions Insurance

Notary errors and omissions insurance provides protection for Notaries who are sued for damages resulting from unintentional notarial mistakes. In the event of a lawsuit, the E&O insurance company will provide and pay for the Notary's legal counsel and absorb any damages levied by a court or agreed to in a settlement, up to the policy coverage limit. Errors and omissions insurance does not, however, protect the Notary in cases of intentional misconduct. ■

As a full-service organization, the National Notary Association makes available to New Jersey Notaries all notarial items required by law, custom and convenience.

10 Most-Asked Questions

Every Notary has a question or two about whether and how to notarize, but there are certain questions that pop up again and again. These top 10 are asked repeatedly at the National Notary Association's seminars, its annual National Conference of Notaries Public and through correspondence with Association members.

As with most questions about notarization, the answer to these 10 is not always a simple "yes" or "no." Rather, the answer is, "It depends."

Here's what every Notary wants to know:

1. Can I notarize a will?

It depends. Laws regarding wills differ from state to state. Some states do not require notarization of wills, while others allow it as one of several witnessing options. Usually, it is not the will itself that is notarized, but accompanying affidavits signed by witnesses. Under specific circumstances, New Jersey law allows an individual to "self-prove" a will before witnesses and a Notary Public (See "Wills," pages 68–69).

A Notary should only notarize a will if clear instructions and a notarial certificate are provided. If the signer of the will is relying on the Notary for advice on how to proceed, the Notary should ask the individual to consult with an attorney.

The danger in notarizing wills is that would-be testators who have drafted their own wills without legal advice may believe that notarization will make their wills legal and valid. However, even when notarized, such homemade wills may be worthless because the testators failed to obtain the proper number of witnesses or omitted important information.

In fact, notarization itself may actually void an otherwise properly executed handwritten (holographic) will, because courts have occasionally held that any writing on the document other than the testator's invalidates the will.

2. Can I notarize for a stranger with no identification?

Yes. If identification of a signer cannot be based on personal knowledge or identification documents (ID cards), a Notary may rely on the oath or affirmation of one personally known credible identifying witness to identify an unknown signer.

If a credible identifying witness is used, the Notary must personally know the credible identifying witness, who, in turn, must personally know the document signer. This establishes a "chain of personal knowledge" from the Notary to the credible identifying witness to the signer.

A credible identifying witness should be someone the Notary believes to be trustworthy and impartial. If a person has a financial or other beneficial interest in a document, that individual could not be a reliable witness.

When no credible identifying witness is available to identify a stranger without IDs, the Notary may have no choice but to tell the signer to find a personally known Notary or a friend who personally knows a Notary.

3. Can I notarize a photograph?

No. To simply stamp and sign a photograph is improper. A Notary's signature and seal (if used) must appear only on a notarial certificate (such as an acknowledgment or jurat) accompanying a written statement signed by another person.

However, a signature on a written statement referring to an accompanying or attached photograph may be notarized; if the photograph is large enough, the statement and notarial certificate might even appear on its reverse side. Such a format may be acceptable when notarized photos are requested by persons seeking medical or health licenses, or by legal resident aliens renewing foreign passports.

A word of caution here: A Notary should always be suspicious about notarizing a photo-bearing card or document that could be used as a bogus "official" ID.

4. What if there's no room for my seal or if it smears?

Usually, if notarial wording printed on a document leaves no room for a seal, a loose certificate can be attached and filled out instead if the certificate wording is substantially the same as on the document.

If an initial seal impression is unreadable and there is ample room on the document, another impression can be affixed nearby. The illegibility of the first impression will indicate why a second seal impression was necessary. The Notary should record in the journal that a second seal was affixed.

A Notary should *never* attempt to fix an imperfect seal impression with a pen, ink or correction fluid. This may be viewed as evidence of tampering and cause the document's rejection by a recorder.

5. Can I notarize signatures on faxes or photocopies of documents?

Yes. A photocopy may be notarized as long as it bears an *original* signature, meaning the photocopy must have been signed with pen and ink. A photocopied signature should *never* be notarized.

Similarly, a faxed document must be signed in ink. In addition, if a faxed document is on thermal paper (the slick paper sometimes used in fax machines), the document should be photocopied onto regular copy paper to avoid the fading of any printed matter and to allow the affixation of signatures and the Notary's seal.

Note that some public recorders may not accept notarized signatures on photocopied documents because they will not adequately reproduce in microfilming.

When carbon copies are made, the Notary will sometimes be asked to "conform" rather than to notarize the copies. To conform a copy, the Notary reaffixes the official seal on the copy (carbon will not readily transfer a seal impression) and writes "Conformed Copy" prominently across the top of the copy.

6. Can I notarize for customers only?

No and yes. As a public official, a Notary is not commissioned to serve just the customers or clients of any one business, even when the employer has paid for the bond, commissioning fees and notarial supplies. There is no such officer as a "Notary Private."

That said, New Jersey law has a provision that allows a Notary employed by a financial institution to refuse to administer oaths and affirmations to any person during business hours, as long as this is the employer's consistent policy. The Notary is not legally required to adhere to these provisions, but, of course, failure to follow any employer's directions or policies may bring certain consequences.

Discrimination against anyone who presents a lawful request for notarization is not a suitable policy for a public official commissioned to serve all of the public equally. Also, such discrimination can provide the basis for lawsuits.

7. Can I notarize a document in a language I can't read?

Yes. As long as the notarial certificate and document signature are in a language the Notary *can* read, New Jersey Notaries are not expressly prohibited from notarizing documents written in languages they *cannot* read.

However, there are certain difficulties and dangers in notarizing documents the Notary cannot read. The main difficulty for the Notary is making an accurate journal description of an unreadable document; the main danger is that the document may be blatantly fraudulent.

In addition, under no circumstances should a notarization be performed if the Notary and the principal signer cannot communicate in the same language.

8. Can I certify a copy of a birth certificate?

No. Some states — although not New Jersey — allow Notaries to certify copies, but copies of documents that are either public records or publicly recordable should never be certified by Notaries. Only an officer in a bureau of vital statistics (see pages 106–110) should certify a copy of a birth certificate or other vital public record; a Notary's "certification" of a birth or death record may actually lend credibility to a counterfeit or altered document. Only a county recording official should certify a copy of a deed or other recordable instrument.

In states allowing Notary-certified copies, the types of documents that Notaries may properly certify copies of are original personal papers such as letters, college diplomas and in-house business documents.

9. Does a document have to be signed in my presence?

No and yes. Documents requiring acknowledgments normally do not need to be signed in the Notary's presence. However, the signer *must appear* before the Notary at the time of notarization to acknowledge having freely signed for the purposes stated in the document.

An acknowledgment certificate indicates that the signer personally appeared before the Notary, was identified by the Notary and acknowledged to the Notary that the document was freely signed.

On the other hand, documents requiring a jurat *must be* signed in the Notary's presence, as dictated by the typical jurat wording, "Subscribed (signed) and sworn to before me ..."

In executing a jurat, a Notary guarantees the signer personally appeared before the Notary, was identified by the Notary, was given an oath or affirmation by the Notary and signed the document in the Notary's presence. Unlike with acknowledgments, Notaries are not required by law to positively identify a signer of a document with jurat wording. However, state officials insist the Notary positively identify the jurat signer in the same manner as for an acknowledgment.

10. Can I notarize for a family member?

Yes and no. Although state law does not directly address notarizing for family members, Notaries who do so may violate the statutes prohibiting a direct beneficial interest — especially in notarizing for spouses in states with community property laws.

Besides the possibility of a financial interest in notarizing for a relative, there may be an "emotional interest" that can prevent the Notary from acting impartially. For example, a Notary who is asked to notarize a contract signed by his brother might attempt to persuade the sibling to sign or not sign. As a brother, the individual is entitled to exert influence — but this is entirely improper for a Notary.

Even if a Notary has no direct beneficial interest in the document and does not attempt to influence the signer, notarizing for a relative could subject the document to a legal challenge if other parties to the transaction allege that the Notary could not have acted impartially. ■

Steps to Proper Notarization

What constitutes reasonable care?

If a Notary can convincingly show that he or she used every reasonable precaution expected of a person of ordinary prudence and intelligence, then the Notary has exercised reasonable care — a shield against liability.

The following 14-step checklist will help Notaries apply reasonable care and avoid the most common pitfalls.

1. Require every signer to personally appear.

The signer *must* appear in person before the Notary on the date and in the county stated in the notarial certificate. "Personal appearance" means the signer is in the Notary's physical presence — face to face in the same room. A telephone call is not acceptable as personal appearance.

2. Make a careful identification.

The Notary should identify every document signer through either personal knowledge, a credible identifying witness under oath or reliable identification documents (ID cards).

When using ID cards, the Notary must examine them closely to detect alteration, counterfeiting or evidence that they have been issued to an impostor. Do not rely on a type of card with which you are unfamiliar, unless you check it against a reference such as the *U.S. Identification Manual* or the *ID Checking Guide*.

3. Feel certain the signer understands the document.

A conscientious Notary will be certain not only of the signer's identity and willingness to sign, but will also make a layperson's judgment about the signer's ability to understand the document. While New Jersey Notaries are not expressly required by law to determine "competence," it is in the Notary's best interest to make a commonsense judgment about the signer's awareness.

A document signer who cannot respond intelligibly in a simple conversation with the Notary should not be considered lucid enough to sign at that moment. If in doubt, the Notary can ask the signer if he or she understands the document and can explain its purpose. Or, if in a medical environment, the signer's doctor can be consulted for a professional opinion.

4. Check the signature.

The Notary must make sure the document signer signs the same name appearing on the identification presented.

To check for possible forgery, the Notary should compare the signature the person leaves in the Notary's journal against the signatures on the document and on the IDs. Also, it should be noted whether the signer appears to be laboring on the journal signature, a possible indication of forgery in progress.

Generally, an abbreviated form of a name (John D. Smith instead of John David Smith, for example) is acceptable. However, deviation is only allowed if the individual is signing with *less* than and not *more* than what is on the identification document.

5. Look for blank spaces.

New Jersey Notaries are not expressly prohibited from notarizing incomplete documents, but documents with blank spaces have a great potential for fraudulent misuse. A borrower, for example, might sign an incomplete promissory note, trusting the lender to fill it out, and then later find that the lender has written in an amount in excess of what was actually borrowed.

If the blanks are inapplicable and intended to be left unfilled, the signer should be asked to line through each space (using ink), or to write in "Not Applicable" or "NA."

6. Scan the document.

Notaries are not required to read the documents they notarize. However, they should note certain important particulars about a document, such as its title, for recording in the journal of notarial acts. Notaries may also count and record the number of pages; this can show whether pages are later fraudulently added or removed.

7. Check the document's date.

For acknowledgments, the date of signing on the document must either *precede or be the same as* the date of the notarization but not follow it. For a jurat, the document signing date and the notarization date *must be the same.*

A document dated to follow the date on its notarial certificate risks rejection by a recorder, who may question how the document could have been notarized before it was signed.

8. Keep a journal of notarial acts.

New Jersey law requires every Notary to take an oath to "keep a true record of all such matters." If a notarized document is lost or altered, or if certain facts about the transaction are later challenged, a Notary's journal becomes valuable evidence. It can protect the rights of all parties to a transaction and help defend the Notary against false accusations.

The Notary should include *all* the pertinent details of the notarization in the journal: the date, time and type of notarization; the date and type of document; the signature, printed name and address of the signer (and any witnesses); how this person was identified; and notarial fees charged, if any. In addition, signers of important documents, such as real property deeds, might also be asked to leave a thumbprint in the Notary's journal, although this is not a legal requirement. Any other pertinent data, such as the capacity the signer is claiming, may also be entered.

9. Complete the journal entry first.

The Notary should complete the journal entry entirely *before* filling out the notarial certificate. This prevents a signer from leaving before the important public record of the notarization is made in the journal.

10. Make sure the document has notarial wording.

If a notarial certificate does not come with the document, the Notary must ask the document signer what type of notarization — acknowledgment, jurat or other — is required. The Notary may then type the appropriate notarial wording on the document or attach a preprinted, "loose" certificate.

If the signer does not know what type of notarization is required, he or she should contact the document's issuing or receiving agency or an attorney to determine this. This decision is *never* the Notary's to make unless the Notary is also an attorney.

11. Be attentive to details.

When filling out the certificate, the Notary needs to make sure the venue correctly identifies the place of notarization; if the venue is preprinted and incorrect, the Notary must line through the incorrect state and/or county, write in the proper site of the notarization and initial the change.

Also, the Notary must pay attention to spaces on the notarial certificate that indicate the number and gender of the document signers, as well as how they were identified — for example, leave the plural "(s)" untouched or cross it out, as appropriate.

12. Affix your signature and seal properly.

Notaries should sign in *exactly* the same name as appears on their commissioning papers. The seal, if used, should be placed as close to the Notary's signature as possible without overprinting it. To prevent illegibility, a Notary seal should not be affixed over wording, particularly over a signature.

New Jersey law does not require Notaries to use seals; however, a Notary must print, type or stamp his or her name next to his or her signature on notarial certificates.

13. Protect 'loose' certificates.

If the Notary must attach a notarial certificate, it should be securely stapled to the left margin of the document. Notaries can protect against the removal of such attachments by embossing them together with the document and writing the particulars of the document to which the certificate is attached on the certificate. For example, the notation, "This certificate is attached to a 15-page partnership agreement between John Smith and Mary Doe, signed November 14, 2005," would deter fraudulent removal and reattachment of a loose certificate.

14. Don't give advice.

Every state prohibits nonattorneys from practicing law. Notaries should *never* prepare or complete documents for others, or give advice on any matter relating to a document unless they are attorneys or professionals certified or licensed in a relevant area of expertise (e.g., real estate). The nonattorney Notary *never* chooses the type of certificate or notarization a document needs, since this decision can have important legal ramifications. The Notary could be held liable for any damages resulting from an incorrectly chosen certificate or notarization. ■

Notary Laws Explained

In layperson's language, this chapter discusses and clarifies key parts of the laws of New Jersey that regulate Notaries Public. Most of these laws are reprinted in full in "New Jersey Laws Pertaining to Notaries Public," beginning on page 81.

THE NOTARY COMMISSION

Application for New Commission

Qualifications. To become a Notary in New Jersey, whether as a first-time Notary or to renew a commission, the applicant: (NJSA 52:7-12; 52:7-13)

1) Must be at least 18 years old.

2) Must be a resident of New Jersey, or be a resident of an adjoining state and maintain a place of business or office in New Jersey.

3) Must not have been convicted in New Jersey or another state of an offense involving dishonesty or of a crime in the first or second degree.

4) Although not a statutory requirement, a Notary Public should be able to read, write, speak, and understand the English language.

Endorsement. The completed application form must be endorsed by a member of the New Jersey Legislature. (NJSA 52:7-11)

Citizenship. U.S. citizenship is not required to become a New Jersey Notary, though any noncitizen applicant should be a legal resident. A 1984 Supreme Court decision, *Bernal v. Fainter*, declared that no state may deny a Notary commission merely on the basis of lack of U.S. citizenship.

Rejection of Application. The State Treasurer may reject an application for a conviction in New Jersey or any other state or U.S. jurisdiction of a crime involving dishonesty (e.g., forgery, counterfeiting) or of a crime of the first or second degree. (NJSA 52:7-20, 52:7-21)

Application Fee. A nonrefundable application fee of $25 shall be submitted with a first-time or renewal application. An additional fee will be required at the time of filing the Notary Public Commission Certificate and Oath Qualification Certificate with the county clerk. (NJSA 52:7-11, 22A:2-29)

Application Misstatement. As stated on the commission application, substantial and material misstatement or omission in the application for a Notary commission is reason for the State Treasurer to deny, revoke, or suspend a Notary's commission.

Qualification as a Delaware Notary. Residents of New Jersey who maintain or are regularly employed in an office in Delaware may qualify for a Delaware Notary commission. For more information, contact: Secretary of State, 401 Federal St., Suite 3, Dover, DE 19901; or call (302) 739-4111.

Qualification as a New York Notary. Residents of New Jersey who maintain or are regularly employed in an office in New York may qualify for a New York Notary commission. For more information, contact: Division of Licensing Services, 84 Holland Ave., Albany, NY 12208-3490; or call (518) 474-4429.

Qualification as a Pennsylvania Notary. Residents of New Jersey who maintain or are regularly employed in an office in Pennsylvania may qualify for a Pennsylvania Notary commission. For more information, contact: Department of State, Bureau of Commissions, Elections and Legislation, Notary Division, 210 North Office Building, Harrisburg, PA 17120; or call (717) 787-5280.

Application for Reappointment

Application. A Notary seeking reappointment must apply for a new commission and follow the same procedures as when applying for a commission for the first time. (NJSA 52:7-11)

Usually — as long as the Notary's address information is correct in the state's records — the State Treasurer will automatically send the Notary a renewal package within three months of the current commission's expiration. However, if not received, the Notary is ultimately responsible for requesting a renewal package if the Notary wants to avoid a gap between commission terms.

Exam

Not Required. An exam is not required to obtain a new or renewed Notary commission. However, a Notary should study and be familiar with the laws of notarization in order to properly perform the duties expected of a Notary.

Notary Bond and Liability

Not Required. New Jersey Notaries are not required to obtain a surety bond.

Liability. As ministerial officials, Notaries generally may be held financially responsible for any and all damages caused by their mistakes or misconduct in performing notarial acts.

If a person is financially injured by a Notary's negligence or failure to properly execute a notarial act — whether performed intentionally or unintentionally — the Notary may be sued in civil court and ordered to pay all resulting damages, including attorneys' fees.

A person need not be named in a document in order to sue a Notary for damages resulting from the Notary's handling of that document. If, for example, a lender accepts a forged, notarized deed as collateral for a loan, the lender might sue to recover losses from the Notary who witnessed the notarized deed.

Penalties for Fraud. Willful violations involving fraud and dishonesty may lead to the revocation of a New Jersey notarial commission. The Notary will also be subject to civil and criminal actions. (NJSA 2C:43-3)

Errors and Omissions Insurance. Up to the policy coverage limit, errors and omissions insurance will absorb a Notary's expenses in defending against a lawsuit caused by a Notary's unintentional mistake.

Oath of Office

Requirement. New Jersey Notaries are required to take and file an oath of office before executing any acts as a Notary Public. (NJSA 52:7-14)

Filing the Oath. The oath must be taken and filed with the clerk of the county in which the Notary resides within three months of the commission start date indicated on the Commission Certificate. Nonresident applicants shall take the oath before the clerk of the county in New Jersey in which the applicant maintains an office or is employed.

To take the oath, the applicant must take the Notary Commission Certificate and Oath Qualification Certificate to the clerk of the county in which the he or she resides or is employed. The clerk will then administer the required oath in which the applicant swears to faithfully and honestly discharge the duties of the office of Notary Public for New Jersey.

Within 10 days after administering the oath, the county clerk returns the Oath Qualification Certificate to the Notary Public Section and records the "sworn date" in the county clerk's files. (NJSA 52:7-14)

A Notary may choose to file additional Qualification Certificates in other counties. Although the Notary has statewide jurisdiction, filing additional certificates makes it easier for a county clerk to authenticate a Notary's commission if the Notary lives and works in different counties. However, filing duplicate Qualification Certificates is not required. (NJSA 52:7-15)

Fee. The county clerk will charge a fee to administer the oath and another fee to file and record it. The Notary applicant should contact the local county clerk to determine these fees. (NJSA 22A:2-29)

Failure to File by Deadline. The State Treasurer will cancel the commission of any Notary Public who fails to take the required oath within three months from the date listed on the Commission Certificate. (NJSA 52:7-14)

Jurisdiction

Statewide. Resident and nonresident (living in an adjoining state and working in New Jersey) New Jersey Notaries may perform official acts throughout the state, but not beyond the state borders. (NJSA 52:7-15)

A Notary may not witness a signing outside of New Jersey and then return to the state to perform the notarization. All parts of a given notarization must be performed at the same time and place within the state of New Jersey.

Term of Office

Five-Year Term. The term of office for a New Jersey Notary Public is five years. Each term begins on the date specified by the State Treasurer on the Commission Certificate and ends at midnight on its commission expiration date or as deemed necessary by the State Treasurer. (NJSA 52:7-11)

Resignation

Notification. To resign, a Notary should submit a written notice to the State Treasurer, giving an effective date. Such a resignation is appropriate if the Notary moves and does not retain a place of business or office in New Jersey. It is recommended the notice be sent by certified mail.

The resignation notice may also be sent to the office of the clerk of the county where the Notary has filed the Commission and Qualification Certificates.

Disposition of Seal and Records. If the resigning Notary has a seal of office or a stamp that he or she used to affix information on certificates, these should be destroyed or defaced to prevent fraudulent use. If the Notary maintained a journal of notarial acts or other recordbook, the State Treasurer recommends the Notary retain the journal or recordbook for a reasonable amount of time to reflect the statute of limitations.

Death of Notary

Notification. If a Notary dies, the Notary's personal representative should notify the State Treasurer. The notification should include the Notary's name and commission number, as well as any additional pertinent information, and should be sent by certified mail.

Disposition of Seal and Records. If the deceased Notary used a seal or stamp to affix information on notarial certificates, these should be destroyed or defaced to prevent fraudulent use. If the Notary maintained a journal or other recordbook, the State Treasurer recommends that the Notary's personal representative retain the journal for a reasonable amount of time that reflects the statute of limitations.

Change of Address

Notification Required. When a Notary changes his or her address, notification must be made to the State Treasurer — and to all county clerks where Qualification Certificates are filed — before notarizing any documents.

Change of address forms are available from: State of New Jersey, Division of Revenue, Notary Public Section, P.O. Box 452, Trenton, NJ 08625; or by calling (609) 292-9292.

The Notary must return the change of address form and a $25 fee (payable to the State Treasurer) by certified mail to the Notary Public Section at the address above.

Change of Name

Notification Required. When a Notary changes his or her name, notification should be made to the State Treasurer — and all county clerks where additional certificates may have been filed — before notarizing any documents. Change of name forms are available from: State of New Jersey, Division of Revenue, Notary Public Section, P.O. Box 452, Trenton, NJ 08625; or by calling (609) 292-9292.

The Notary should return the change of name form and a $25 fee (payable to the State Treasurer), by certified mail to the address above. (NJSA 52:7-18)

Retaining the Commission. A New Jersey Notary who files a change of name form with the State Treasurer also may request a new Commission Certificate indicating the new name, though this is not required.

The request should be made when filing the name change form and must be accompanied by a $1 fee, in addition to the $25 fee for filing the name change. Once a name change form has been filed — whether or not a new Commission Certificate is obtained — the Notary must notarize using the new name. (NJSA 52:7-18)

Commissioner of Deeds

Appointment. A nonresident commissioner of deeds for New Jersey may be appointed by the State Treasurer as necessary, except where such appointment is incompatible with the laws of the state in which the commissioner resides. (NJSA 52:6-12)

Such "foreign" commissioners of deeds may also accept an appointment in an adjoining state while residing in New Jersey. (NJSA 52:6-15)

Application. A person may apply for appointment as a foreign commissioner of deeds on a form prescribed by the State Treasurer. As with a Notary commission, the application must be endorsed by a member of the Legislature, the Secretary of State, or the Assistant Secretary of State. Renewal shall be made in the same manner as with the original application. (NJSA 52:6-12)

Fee. The State Treasurer will charge a $25 fee to file a certificate of appointment as a commissioner of deeds. Fees are payable to the State Treasurer. (NJSA 52:6-16)

Term of Office. The term of office for a New Jersey commissioner of deeds is three years and is subject to removal by the Governor. (NJSA 52:6-13)

Change of Residence. If a commissioner of deeds moves out of the state, territory, or district in which he or she resides at the time of appointment, the commission will be void. (NJSA 52:6-14)

Oath Required. Each person appointed as a commissioner of deeds must take an oath to faithfully perform the duties of the office. The oath may be administered by a Notary Public or other public officer authorized to administer oaths, and must be filed with the State Treasurer. (NJSA 52:6-17, 52:6-18)

Seal Required. Unlike Notaries Public, a commissioner of deeds is required to use a seal and file a copy of it with the State Treasurer. (NJSA 52:6-18, 52:6-20)

OFFICIAL NOTARIAL ACTS

Authorized Acts

Notaries may perform the following official acts:

• Acknowledgments, certifying that a signer personally appeared before the Notary, was identified by the Notary, and acknowledged freely signing the document. (See pages 30–33.) (NJSA 46:14-6.1)

• Depositions, certifying that the spoken words of a witness were accurately taken down in writing, though this act is most often done by skilled court reporters. (See pages 34–36.) (NJ Rules of Civil Practice, Rule 4:12, Section 4:12-1)

• Affidavits, administration of an oath or affirmation in conjunction with a person's signed statement. (See pages 34–36.) (NJSA 41:2-17)

• Jurats, as found in affidavits and other sworn

documents, certifying that the signer personally appeared before the Notary, signed in the Notary's presence, and took an oath or affirmation from the Notary. (See pages 36–37.) (NJSA 41:2-17)

• <u>Oaths and Affirmations</u>, which are solemn promises to God (oath) or solemn promises on one's own personal honor (affirmation). (See pages 37–39.) (NJSA 41:2-1, 41:2-17)

• <u>Proofs of Execution</u>, certifying that a subscribing witness personally appeared and swore to the Notary that another person, the principal, signed a document. (See pages 39–41.) (NJSA 46:14-6.1)

• <u>Protests</u>, certifying that a written promise to pay, such as a bill of exchange, was not honored. (See pages 41–43.) (NJSA 2A:82-7)

• <u>Witnessing a Safe Deposit Box Opening</u>, by a bank or other safe deposit box owner, must be witnessed by a Notary. (See pages 43–44.) (NJSA 17:14A-51)

Unauthorized Acts

<u>Certified Copies</u>. A certified copy is a verified exact duplicate of an original document. A New Jersey Notary is not expressly authorized by law to issue certified copies.

Requests for certified copies should be directed to the agency that holds or issued the original. For certified copies of birth, death, or marriage certificates, and other vital records, the person requesting the copy should be referred to the Bureau of Vital Statistics (or the equivalent) in the state where the event occurred. (See "Bureaus of Vital Statistics," pages 106–110.)

An alternative to a Notary-certified copy is copy certification by document custodian. Here the permanent keeper of a document — the custodian — certifies the duplicate in a written statement, and the Notary executes a jurat for the custodian's signature. (See "Copy Certification by Document Custodian," pages 33–34.)

Marriages. New Jersey Notaries have no authority to perform marriages unless they are also ministers. Only Notaries in Maine, South Carolina, and Florida are empowered to perform marriages strictly by virtue of holding a notarial commission. (See "Weddings," page 70.)

Notary's Own Signature. Although the practice is not expressly prohibited by law, the New Jersey State Treasurer directs Notaries not to notarize their own signatures.

Telephone Notarizations. Notarizations over the telephone are absolutely forbidden. State law requires that a document signer personally appear before the Notary, face to face in the same room, at the time of the notarization, not before, not after. (NJSA 46:14-2.1)

Acknowledgments

A Common Notarial Act. Acknowledgments are one of the most common forms of notarization. Typically, they are executed on deeds and other documents affecting real property that will be publicly recorded by a county official. (NJSA 46:14-2.1)

Purpose. In executing an acknowledgment, a Notary certifies three things: (NJSA 46:14-2.1)

1) The signer *personally appeared* before the Notary on the date and in the county indicated on the notarial certificate (notarization cannot be based on a telephone call or on a Notary's familiarity with a signature).

2) The signer was *positively identified* by the Notary through either personal knowledge or satisfactory evidence (see "Identifying Document Signers," pages 44–48).

3) The signer *acknowledged* to the Notary that the signature was freely made for the purposes stated in the document. (If a document is willingly signed in the presence of the Notary, this tacit act can serve just as well as an oral statement of acknowledgment.)

Certificate for Acknowledgment. For every acknowledgment, the Notary must complete, sign and seal (if a seal is used) an appropriate certificate of acknowledgment. (NJSA 46:14-2.1)

The certificate wording may either be preprinted or typed at the end of the document, or appear as an attachment (a "loose certificate") that is stapled to the document's signature page. (NJSA 2A:82-17, 46:14-2.1)

Unlike most states, New Jersey statutes do not prescribe acknowledgment certificate wording that Notaries must use. However, the on-line edition of the *New Jersey Notary Public Manual* offers an example of an acknowledgment certificate with basic wording, not prohibiting use of any other appropriate wording:

State of New Jersey)
) ss.
County of _____)

On _____, 20___, before me, _____, a Notary Public in and for said county, personally appeared _____ (name[s] of signer[s]), who has/have satisfactorily identified himself/herself/ themselves as the signer(s) or/witness(es) to the above-referenced instrument.

Notary Signature _____   (Notary's Seal)
Date _____
My Commission Expires _____

Identification of Acknowledger. In executing an acknowledgment, the Notary must identify the signer through personal knowledge, a credible identifying witness or, identification documents. (See "Identifying Document Signers," pages 44–48.)

Witnessing Signature Not Required. For an acknowledgment, the document does *not* have to be signed in the Notary's presence; however, the signer must appear before the Notary at the time of notarization to *acknowledge having signed* the document. (NJSA 46:14-2.1)

A document could have been signed an hour before, a week before, a year before, etc. — as long as the signer appears before the Notary with the signed document at the time of notarization to admit that the signature is his or her own. (Conversely, for a jurat, requiring an oath or affirmation, the document must be signed in the presence of the Notary. See "Jurats," pages 36–37.)

Terminology. In discussing acknowledgments, it is important to use proper terms. A Notary *takes* or *executes* an acknowledgment, while a document signer *makes* or *gives* an acknowledgment.

Who May Take. Notaries and the following officials of New Jersey and of other U.S. states and foreign jurisdictions may take acknowledgments and proofs within their respective jurisdictions: (NJSA 46:14-6.1, 46:14-8)

1) An attorney at law;

2) A county clerk or deputy county clerk;

3) A register or deputy register of deeds;

4) A surrogate or deputy surrogate;

5) Any officer of the United States or of a foreign nation;

6) A foreign commissioner of deeds for New Jersey, within the jurisdiction of the commission;

7) A foreign service or consular officer or any other representative of the United States to any foreign nation, within the territory of that nation;

8) Any master of the Superior Court;

9) Any public ambassador, minister, consul, vice-consul, consular agent, or charge d'affaires;

10) Any court of law of a foreign jurisdiction; or

11) Any commissioner for oaths, mayor, or chief magistrate.

False Acknowledgments. A Notary must ensure a certificate for an acknowledgment reflects the date the signer actually appeared before the Notary. A certificate that indicates a different date than when the signer actually appeared is fraudulent and possible evidence of a criminal act.

Copy Certification by Document Custodian

Purpose. Because New Jersey Notaries are not specifically allowed to certify copies, copy certification by document custodian may serve as an acceptable alternative when a Notary-certified copy (permitted in many other states and countries) is requested. However, because copy certification by document custodian may not be acceptable to the individual or agency receiving the copy, the person requesting the act should verify it will serve the required purpose.

Procedure. The permanent keeper of the document — the document custodian — certifies the copy, *not* the Notary. The custodian makes a photocopy of the original document; makes a written statement about the trueness, correctness and completeness of the copy; signs that statement before a Notary; and takes an oath or affirmation regarding the truth of the statement. The Notary, having witnessed the signing and given the oath or affirmation, typically executes a jurat.

Not for Vital Records. Copy certification by document custodian is not appropriate for vital records — such as birth, marriage and death certificates — since originals of these documents are retained by public agencies. Persons requesting certified copies of vital records should be directed to the agency that holds the original — typically, the Bureau of Vital Statistics or County Clerk in the area where the birth, death or marriage occurred. (See "Bureaus of Vital Statistics," pages 106–110.)

Certificate for Copy Certification by Document Custodian. In addition to the jurat certificate, a statement by the custodian — attesting to the truth and accuracy of the document — is required. Although not prescribed by law, this format — which includes the required jurat — is recommended by the National Notary Association:

State of New Jersey   )
) ss.
County of _____   )

I, _____ (name of custodian of original document), hereby swear (or affirm) that the attached reproduction of _____ (description of original document) is a true, correct and complete photocopy of a document in my possession.

_____ (signature of custodian) _____ (address)

Subscribed and sworn (or affirmed) before me this _____ day of _____ (month), _____ (year), by _____ (name of custodian).

_____ (Notary's Signature)   (Notary's Seal)

Depositions and Affidavits

Purpose. A deposition is a signed transcript of the signer's oral statements taken down for use in a judicial proceeding. The deposition signer is called the *deponent.*

An affidavit is a signed statement made under oath or affirmation by a person called an *affiant,* and it may be used for a variety of purposes, both in and out of court.

For both a deposition and an affidavit, the Notary must administer an oath or affirmation and complete some form of jurat, which the Notary signs and seals.

Depositions. With a deposition, both sides in a lawsuit or court case have the opportunity to cross-examine the deponent. Questions and answers are then transcribed into a written statement. Used only in judicial proceedings, a deposition is typically signed and sworn to before an oath-administering official. (NJSA 41:2-1, 41:2-17)

New Jersey Notaries have the power to take depositions — meaning, to transcribe the words spoken aloud by a deponent — but this duty is most often executed by trained and certified shorthand reporters, also known as court reporters. While most Notaries do not have the stenographic skills necessary to transcribe a deponent's words, any Notary is competent to administer an oath (or affirmation) or to execute a jurat on an existing deposition. (NJSA 41:2-1 and NJ Rules of Civil Practice, Rule 4:12, Section 4:12-1)

Affidavits. Affidavits are used in and out of court for a variety of purposes, from declaring losses to an insurance company to declaring U.S. citizenship before traveling to a foreign country. An affidavit is a document containing a statement voluntarily signed and sworn to or affirmed before a Notary or other official with oath-administering powers. If used in a judicial proceeding, only one side in the case need participate in the execution of the affidavit, in contrast to the deposition. (NJSA 41:2-1, 41:2-17)

In an affidavit, the Notary's certificate typically sandwiches the affiant's signed statement, with the venue and affiant's name at the top of the document and the jurat wording at the end. The Notary is responsible for the venue and any notarial text at the beginning and end of the affidavit, and the affiant is responsible for the signed statement in the middle.

Certificate for Depositions and Affidavits. Depositions and affidavits require jurat certificates. (See "Jurats," pages 36–37.)

Oath (Affirmation) for Depositions and Affidavits. If no other wording is prescribed in a given instance, a Notary may use the following language in administering an oath (or affirmation) for an affidavit or deposition:

> Do you solemnly swear that the statements made in this affidavit (or deposition) are the truth, the whole truth, and nothing but the truth, so help you God?
>
> (Do you solemnly affirm that the statements made in this affidavit [or deposition] are the truth, the whole truth, and nothing but the truth?)

Response Required. For both oath and affirmation, the

affiant must respond aloud and affirmatively, with "I do" or similar words.

Jurats

Part of Verification. In notarizing affidavits, depositions and other forms of written verification requiring an oath by the signer, the Notary normally executes a jurat.

Purpose. While the purpose of an acknowledgment is to positively identify a document signer, the purpose of a verification with jurat is to compel truthfulness by appealing to the signer's conscience and fear of criminal penalties for perjury.

In executing a jurat, a Notary certifies that:

1) The signer *personally appeared* before the Notary at the time of notarization on the date and in the county indicated (notarization based on a telephone call or on familiarity with a signature is not acceptable);

2) The Notary *watched the signature* being made at the time of notarization; and

3) The Notary *administered an oath* or affirmation to the signer.

Certificate for a Jurat. A typical jurat is the wording, "Subscribed and sworn to (or affirmed) before me on this _____ (date) by _____ (name of signer)..." or similar language. "Subscribed" means "signed."

When jurat wording is not prescribed in a given instance, the National Notary Association recommends the following:

State of New Jersey   )
) ss.
County of _____   )

Subscribed and sworn to (or affirmed) before me this _____ day of _____ (month), _____ (year), by _____ (name of signer).

_____ (Notary's Signature)   (Notary's Seal)

Identification. Unlike Notary-regulators in many states, New Jersey officials direct that a signer of a document requiring a jurat must be positively identified by the Notary through identification documents, personal knowledge, or a credible identifying witness.

Wording for Jurat Oath (Affirmation). If not otherwise prescribed by law, a New Jersey Notary may use the following or similar words to administer an oath (or affirmation) in conjunction with a jurat:

> Do you solemnly swear that the statements in this document are true to the best of your knowledge and belief, so help you God?

> (Do you solemnly affirm that the statements in this document are true to the best of your knowledge and belief?)

Oath or Affirmation Must Be Administered. A Notary Public does not execute a jurat by merely asking a person whether or not the signature on an affidavit is that of the signer. An oath or affirmation must be administered and the affixation of the signature observed by the Notary. (NJSA 41:2-17)

Oaths and Affirmations

Purpose. An oath is a solemn, spoken pledge to a Supreme Being. An affirmation is a solemn, spoken pledge on one's own personal honor, with no reference to a Supreme Being. Both are usually a promise of truthfulness or fidelity and have the same legal effect.

In taking an oath or affirmation in an official proceeding, a person may be subject to criminal penalties for perjury should he or she fail to be truthful.

An oath or affirmation can be a full-fledged notarial act in its own right, as when giving an oath of office to a public official ("swearing in" a public official), or it can be part of the process of notarizing a document (e.g., executing a jurat, or swearing in a credible identifying witness).

A person who objects to taking an oath — pledging to a Supreme Being — may instead be given an affirmation. (NJSA 41:1-6)

Power to Administer. New Jersey Notaries and certain other officers are authorized to administer any oath or affirmation required by state law. (NJSA 41:2-1, 41:2-17)

Wording for Oath (Affirmation). If law does not dictate otherwise, a New Jersey Notary may use the following or similar words in administering an oath (or affirmation):

• Oath (Affirmation) for affiant signing an affidavit or deposition:

Do you solemnly swear that the statements made in this affidavit (or deposition) are the truth, the whole truth, and nothing but the truth, so help you God?

(Do you solemnly affirm that the statements made in this affidavit [or deposition] are the truth, the whole truth, and nothing but the truth?)

• Oath (Affirmation) for credible identifying witness(es):

Do you solemnly swear that you know the signer truly is the person he/she claims to be, so help you God?

(Do you solemnly affirm that you know the signer truly is the person he/she claims to be?)

Response Required. The person taking the oath or affirmation must respond by repeating these words or answering affirmatively with, "I do," "Yes," or similar words. A nod or grunt is not a clear and sufficient response. If a person is unable to speak, the Notary may rely on written notes to communicate.

Ceremony and Gestures. To impress upon the oath-taker or affirmant the importance of truthfulness, the Notary is encouraged to lend a sense of ceremony and formality to the oath or affirmation. During administration of the oath or affirmation, the Notary and the document signer traditionally raise their right hands, though this is not a legal requirement. Notaries generally have discretion to use words and gestures they feel will most compellingly appeal to the conscience of the oath-taker or affirmant.

Prohibited Acts. Only an individual may take an oath (or affirmation). An "artificial person" such as a corporation or a partnership may not take an oath, though a person representing a corporation, partnership or other legal entity may take an oath as an individual, swearing that he or she has the authority to sign for the entity.

An oath (or affirmation) may not be given over the telephone. The oath-taker must physically appear in front of the Notary. In addition, a Notary may not administer an oath (or affirmation) to himself or herself.

Notary/Employer Agreement to Limit Services. A Notary Public employed by a financial institution may agree to the employer's policy which provides that the Notary shall not administer oaths except in the course of business and during the normal business hours of the employer.

A "financial institution" is defined by law as a state or federally chartered bank, savings bank, savings and loan association, or credit union. (NJSA 41:2-3)

Proof of Execution by Subscribing Witness

Purpose. In executing a proof of execution by subscribing witness, a Notary certifies that the signature of a person who does not appear before the Notary — the principal signer — is genuine and freely made based on the sworn testimony of another person who does appear — a subscribing (signing) witness. (NJSA 46:14-2.1)

Proofs of execution are used when the principal signer is out of town or otherwise unavailable to appear before a Notary. Because of their high potential for fraudulent abuse, proofs of execution are not universally accepted, though they are legal for the New Jersey Notary to perform.

That said, New Jersey state officials discourage the use of proofs of execution by subscribing witness. These types of proofs should only be used as a last resort and never merely because the principal signer prefers not to take the time to personally appear before a Notary.

In Lieu of Acknowledgment. On recordable documents, a proof of execution by a subscribing witness is usually regarded as an acceptable substitute for an acknowledgment.

Subscribing Witness. A subscribing witness is a person who watches a principal sign a document (or who personally takes the principal's acknowledgment) and then subscribes (signs) his or her own name on the document at the principal's request. This witness brings that document to a Notary on the principal's behalf and takes an oath or affirmation from the Notary to the effect that the principal did willingly sign (or acknowledge signing) the document and requested the witness to also sign the document. (NJSA 46:14-2.1)

The ideal subscribing witness personally knows the principal signer and has no personal beneficial or financial interest in the document or transaction. It would be foolish of the Notary, for example, to rely on the word of a subscribing witness presenting for notarization a power of attorney naming that very witness as attorney in fact.

Identifying Subscribing Witness. Since the Notary is relying entirely on the word of the subscribing witness to vouch for an absent signer's identity and willingness to sign, it is best for subscribing witnesses to be personally known to the Notary, and this is strongly recommended by Notary regulators. New Jersey law, however, allows the Notary to identify a subscribing witness through identification documents or a credible identifying witness. (NJSA 46:14-2.1)

Certificate for Proof of Execution. New Jersey statute does not prescribe a notarial certificate for a proof of execution by a subscribing witness, though it does specify that the witness must swear that he or she saw the principal signer execute the document. (NJSA 46:14-2.1)

Previous editions of the *New Jersey Notary Public Manual* prescribed the following certificate for a proof of execution by subscribing witness:

State of New Jersey   )
) ss.
County of _____   )

On _____ (date), before me, _____, Notary
Public in and for said county, personally appeared
_____ (name[s] of subscribing witness[es]),
personally known to me (or proved to me on the oath of
_____ [name of credible identifying witness]) to be
the person(s) whose name(s) is/are subscribed on the attached
document as witness(es) thereto, and who, being duly sworn
by me, say(s) that he/she saw _____ (name of absent
principal), sign the attached document, and that said affiant(s)
subscribed his/her/their name(s) to the attached document at
the request of _____ (name of absent principal).

Notary Signature _____   (Notary's Seal)
Date _____
My Commission Expires _____

Oath (Affirmation) for a Subscribing Witness. An
acceptable oath for the subscribing witness might be:

> Do you solemnly swear that you saw (name of the document
> signer) sign his/her name to this document and/or that he/she
> acknowledged to you having executed it for the purposes
> therein stated, so help you God?

> (Do you solemnly affirm that you saw [name of the document
> signer] sign his/her name to this document and/or that he/she
> acknowledged to you having executed it for the purposes
> therein stated?)

The subscribing witness then signs the Notary's journal
or recordbook, and the Notary completes a proof of
execution by subscribing witness certificate, often called a
witness jurat.

Proof of Acknowledgment by Handwriting. In very
limited situations, a proof of acknowledgment by
handwriting may be taken. If a document cannot be
acknowledged or proved for any reason, it may be
proved in Superior Court by proof of handwriting.
(NJSA 46:14-4.1)

Protests
Purpose. In rare instances, Notaries may be asked to
protest a negotiable instrument for nonpayment. A protest

is a written statement by a Notary or other authorized officer verifying that payment was not received on a negotiable instrument such as a bank draft. Failure to pay is called *dishonor.*

Before issuing a certificate of protest, the Notary must present the bank draft or other instrument to the person or entity obligated to pay, a procedure called *presentment.* (NJSA 2A:82-7)

Protest of instruments held by bank or corporation by Notary officer or employee is permitted. (NJSA 7:5-6)

Antiquated Act. In the 19th century, protests were common notarial acts in the United States, but they are rarely performed today due to the advent of modern electronic communications and resulting changes in our banking and financial systems. Modern Notaries most often encounter protests in the context of international commerce.

Special Knowledge Required. Notarial acts of protest are complicated and varied, requiring a special knowledge of financial and legal terminology. Only Notaries who have the requisite knowledge, or who are acting under the supervision of an experienced bank officer or an attorney familiar with the Uniform Commercial Code, should attempt a protest.

Fee. A Notary may charge $2 for executing a protest. For each additional notice of protest delivered in person or by mail, a Notary may charge $0.10 in addition to postage fees. (NJSA 22A:4-13)

Certificate for Protest. A Notary shall provide a certificate to the person requesting a protest. The certificate should include the following information: (NJSA 7:5-3, 7:5-4)

1) The time and place of presentment of the bill or note;

2) The name of the party to whom demand of payment was made; and

3) A copy of the notice of nonpayment, including how, when and where it was served.

Notary's Record of Protests Required. Every Notary Public, upon protesting any bill of exchange or promissory note, must record in a recordbook the time, place and name of the person upon whom demand of payment was made, with a copy of the notice of nonpayment, how and when served; or if sent, in what manner and the time when. If sent by mail, the record must include to whom presentment was directed, the address, and when the notice was deposited at the post office. The Notary's signature must also be on the record. (NJSA 7:5-3)

Witnessing Safe Deposit Box Opening
May Witness Opening. If the rental fee on a safe deposit box, vault, or receptacle has not been paid for one year, and the bank or safe deposit box owner has attempted to contact the lessee without success, the bank may open and inventory the box in the presence of a Notary Public and one of the institution's officers.

Procedure. The Notary issues a certificate stating the lessee's name, the date of the opening, and a list of the contents in the box. The Notary then delivers the certificate to the institution. Within 10 days of the opening, a copy of the certificate must be mailed by the owner of the safe deposit box to the lessee's last known address. (NJSA 17:14A-51)

Certificate for Inventorying a Safe Deposit Box. New Jersey law does not provide specific wording for the certificate. The National Notary Association recommends the following wording:

State of New Jersey   )
) ss.
County of _____)

On the _____ (day) of _____ (month), _____ (year), safe deposit box number _____, rented in the name

of _____, was opened by _____ (name of financial institution) in my presence and in the presence of _____ (name of financial institution officer). The contents of the box consisted of the following:
(list of contents)

_____ (Signature of financial institution officer)
_____ (Print or type name)
_____ (Signature of Notary)   (Notary's Seal)
_____ (Name of Notary, printed, typed or stamped)

PRACTICES AND PROCEDURES

Identifying Document Signers

<u>Acknowledgments</u>. In taking the acknowledgment of a signature on any document, New Jersey law requires the Notary to identify the acknowledger. (NJSA 46:14-2.1)

The following three methods of identification are generally acceptable:

1) The Notary's *personal knowledge* of the signer's identity (See "Personal Knowledge of Identity" below);

2) The oath or affirmation of a personally known *credible identifying witness* (See "Credible Identifying Witnesses," pages 45–46); or

3) Reliable *identification documents* or ID cards (See "Identification Documents," pages 46–48).

<u>Identification for Other Notarial Acts</u>. Unlike most states, New Jersey Notary officials require that *any* signer — for acknowledgments, jurats or other notarial act — be positively identified by the Notary through ID documents, personal knowledge, or one credible identifying witness.

Personal Knowledge of Identity

<u>Definition</u>. The safest and most reliable method of identifying a document signer is for the Notary to depend on his or her own personal knowledge of the signer's identity. Personal knowledge means familiarity with an individual resulting from interactions with that person over a period of time sufficient to eliminate every

reasonable doubt that the person has the identity claimed. The familiarity should come from association with the individual in relation to other people and should be based upon a chain of circumstances surrounding the individual.

New Jersey law does not specify how long a Notary must be acquainted with an individual before personal knowledge of identity may be claimed. The Notary's common sense must prevail. In general, the longer the Notary is acquainted with a person, and the more interactions the Notary has had with that person, the more likely the individual is indeed personally known.

For instance, the Notary might safely regard a friend since childhood as personally known, but the Notary would be foolish to consider a person met for the first time the previous day as such. Whenever the Notary has a reasonable doubt about a signer's identity, that individual should be considered not personally known, and the identification should be made through other acceptable methods: either a credible identifying witness or reliable identification documents.

Credible Identifying Witness(es)

Purpose. When a document signer is not personally known to the Notary and is not able to present reliable ID cards, that signer may be identified on the oath (or affirmation) of one or more credible identifying witnesses.

Qualifications. Every credible identifying witness must personally know the document signer. The credible identifying witness also must be personally known by the Notary. This establishes a "chain of personal knowledge" from the Notary to the credible identifying witness to the signer. In a sense, a credible identifying witness is a walking, talking ID card.

A credible identifying witness should have a reputation for honesty. The witness should be a competent, independent individual who won't be tricked, cajoled, bullied, or otherwise influenced into identifying someone he or she does not really know. In addition, the witness should have no direct personal interest in the transaction requiring a notarial act.

Oath (Affirmation) for Credible Identifying Witness.
The Notary must administer an oath or affirmation to
the credible identifying witness in order to
compel truthfulness.

If not otherwise prescribed by law, the following or
similar wording may be used by a New Jersey Notary:

> Do you solemnly swear that you know the signer is the
> person he/she claims to be, so help you God?
>
> (Do you solemnly affirm that you know the signer is the
> person he/she claims to be?)

Signature in Notary's Journal. If the Notary maintains
a journal, each credible identifying witness should sign
the Notary's journal, along with the document signer.
The Notary should also print each witness's name
and address.

Not a Subscribing Witness. Do not confuse *credible
identifying* witness with *subscribing* witness. A credible
identifying witness vouches for the identity of a signer
who appears before the Notary. A subscribing witness
vouches for the genuineness of the signature of a person
who does not appear before the Notary. (See "Proof of
Execution by Subscribing Witness," pages 39–41.)

Identification Documents (ID Cards)

Acceptable Identification Documents. Notaries
customarily are allowed to use reliable identification
documents (ID cards) to identify document signers whom
they do not personally know. Such cards are considered
to be "satisfactory evidence" of identity in lieu of personal
knowledge, just as is the sworn word of a personally
known credible identifying witness.

The National Notary Association urges Notaries to
rely only on IDs with a photograph, a physical
description (e.g., "brown hair, green eyes"), and a
signature of the bearer. Most government-issued IDs
contain all three components.

Examples of acceptable forms of identification include:

1) New Jersey driver's license or official nondriver's ID.

2) U.S. or foreign passport.

3) U.S. military ID.

4) Resident alien ID, or "green card," issued by the U.S. Bureau of Citizenship and Immigration Services (BCIS).

Multiple Identification. While one good identification document or card may be sufficient to identify a signer, the Notary may always ask for more, especially if the Notary has reasons to suspect that the signer has fraudulent identification.

Unacceptable Identification Documents. Because they are easily counterfeited, Social Security cards, birth certificates, and credit cards are worthless as primary identifying documents.

Fraudulent Identification. Identification documents are the least secure of the three methods of identifying a document signer, because phony ID cards are common. The Notary should scrutinize each card for evidence of tampering or counterfeiting, or for evidence that it is a genuine card that has been issued to an impostor.

Some clues that an ID card may have been fraudulently tampered with include: mismatched type styles; a photograph with a raised surface; a signature that does not match the signature on the document; unauthorized lamination of the card; and smudges, erasures, smears and discolorations.

Possible tip-offs to a counterfeit ID card include: misspelled words, a brand new-looking card with an old date of issuance, two cards with exactly the same photograph showing the bearer in identical clothing or with an identical background, and inappropriate patterns and features.

Some possible indications that an identification card may have been issued to an impostor include: the birthdate or address on the card is unfamiliar to the bearer, all the ID cards seem brand new, and the bearer is unwilling to leave a thumbprint in the journal. (Such a print is not required by law but is requested by some Notaries as protection against forgers and lawsuits. Refusal to leave a thumbprint is not in itself grounds to deny a notarization.)

Journal of Notarial Acts

Recommended. Since New Jersey statute stipulates that each Notary must take an oath of office swearing "that he will make and keep a true record of all such matters as are required by law," the National Notary Association recommends that each Notary maintain a recordbook or official notarial journal chronicling all notarial acts. (NJSA 2A:82-6, 52:7-14)

However, New Jersey law does specifically require Notaries to maintain a record of protests, including all pertinent information relating to the execution of protests. (NJSA 7:5-3)

Nothing prevents a Notary from recording *all* notarizations in a journal, log, or recordbook. Of course, the National Notary Association and many Notary-regulating officials across the nation strongly endorse the policy of keeping a journal of all notarial acts as both protection for the public and the Notary.

Prudent Notaries keep detailed and accurate journals of their notarial acts for many reasons:

• Keeping records is a *businesslike practice* that every conscientious businessperson and public official should engage in. Not keeping records of important transactions, whether private or public, is risky.

• A Notary's recordbook *protects the public's rights* to valuable property and to due process by providing documentary evidence in the event a document is lost or altered, or if a transaction is later challenged.

• In the event of a civil lawsuit alleging that the Notary's negligence or misconduct caused the plaintiff serious financial harm, a detailed journal of notarial acts can *protect the Notary* by showing that reasonable care was used to identify a signer. It would be difficult to contend that the Notary did not bother to identify a signer if the Notary's journal contains a detailed description of the ID cards that the signer presented.

• Since civil lawsuits arising from a contested notarial act typically occur three to six years after the act occurs, the Notary normally cannot accurately testify in court about the particulars of a notarization without a journal to *aid the Notary's memory.*

• Journals of notarial acts *prevent or abort baseless lawsuits* by showing that a Notary did use reasonable care, or that a transaction did occur as recorded. Journal fingerprints and signatures are especially effective in defeating such groundless suits.

• Requiring each document signer to leave a signature — or even a fingerprint — in the Notary's journal both *deters attempted forgeries* and provides strong evidence for a conviction should a forgery occur.

Journal Entries. The Notary's recordbook should contain the following information for each notarial act performed:

1) The date, time of day, and type of notarization (e.g., jurat, acknowledgment, etc.).

2) The type (or title) of document notarized (e.g., deed of trust, affidavit of support, etc.), including the number of pages and the date of the document.

3) The signature, address, and printed name of each document signer and witness.

4) A statement as to how the signer's identity was confirmed (If by personal knowledge, the journal entry should read "Personal Knowledge." If by satisfactory evidence, the journal entry must contain either: a description of the ID card accepted, including the type of ID, the government agency issuing the ID, the serial or identifying number, and the date of issuance or

expiration; the signature of any credible identifying witness and how that credible identifying witness was identified — see "Credible Identifying Witness(es)," pages 45–46).

5) Any other pertinent information, including the fee charged for the notarial service or any peculiarities relating to the signer or the document.

Journal Thumbprint. Increasingly, Notaries are asking document signers to leave a thumbprint in the journal. The journal thumbprint is a strong deterrent to forgery, because it represents absolute proof of the forger's identity and that the signer did, indeed, appear before the Notary. Nothing prevents a Notary from asking for a thumbprint for every notarial act, if the signer is willing. However, the Notary may not make leaving a thumbprint a precondition for notarizing.

Completing Entry Before Certificate. The Notary should complete the journal entry before filling out the notarial certificate on a document. This prevents the signer from leaving with the notarized document before vital information can be entered in the journal.

Never Surrender Journal. Notaries should never surrender control of their journals to anyone, unless expressly subpoenaed by a court order. Even when an employer has paid for the Notary's official journal and seal, they go with the Notary upon termination of employment.

No person but the Notary may properly possess and use these records. This also means that a Notary should not share his or her official journal with another person, even if the other person also is a Notary. The journal should always be in the exclusive control of the Notary named in it.

Notarial Certificate

Requirement. In notarizing any document, a Notary must complete a notarial certificate. The certificate is wording that indicates exactly what the Notary has certified. The notarial certificate may be either preprinted or typed on the document itself or as an attachment to it. The certificate should contain: (NJSA 2A:82-17, 46:14-2.1)

1) A *venue* indicating where the notarization is being performed. "State of New Jersey, County of _____," is the typical venue wording, with the county name inserted in the blank. The letters "SS." or "SCT." sometimes appear after the venue; they abbreviate the traditional Latin word *scilicet*, meaning "in particular" or "namely."

2) A *statement of particulars* which indicates what the notarization has attested. An acknowledgment certificate might include such wording as: "On _____ (date) before me, _____ (name of Notary), personally appeared, _____ (name of signer), personally known to me (or proved to me on the basis of satisfactory evidence) to be the person(s)...etc." A jurat certificate would include such wording as: "Subscribed and sworn to (or affirmed) before me this _____ (date) by _____ (name of signer)."

3) A *testimonium clause*, which may be optional if the date is included in the statement of particulars: "Witness my hand and official seal, this the ____ day of _____ (month), ____ (year)." In this short sentence, the Notary formally attests to the truthfulness of the preceding facts in the certificate. "Hand" means signature.

4) The *official signature of the Notary*, exactly as the name appears on the Notary's commissioning paper.

5) The *seal of the Notary*, although not required by New Jersey law. On many certificates the letters "L.S." appear, indicating where the seal is to be located. These letters abbreviate the Latin term *locus sigilli*, meaning "place of the seal." An inking seal should be placed near but not over the letters, so that wording imprinted by the seal will not be obscured. An embossing seal

may be placed directly over the letters — slightly displacing portions of the characters and leaving a clue that document examiners can use to distinguish an original from a forged photocopy.

6) Depending on state law, additional information — similar in content to the information in a Notary's seal — is sometimes required. In addition to his or her official signature, New Jersey *does* require the Notary to print, type or stamp an impression of the Notary's name. (NJSA 52:7-19)

New Jersey Notaries who use seals also may consider including the title of their office ("Notary Public"), their jurisdiction ("State of New Jersey") and their commission expiration date.

Loose Certificates. When certificate wording is not preprinted on the document for the Notary to fill out, a "loose" certificate may be attached by the Notary. This form is typically stapled to the left margin of the signature page. Only one side of the certificate should be stapled, so it can be lifted to view the document.

To prevent a loose certificate from being removed and fraudulently placed on another document, there are precautions a Notary can take. The Notary can emboss the certificate and document together, writing, "Attached document bears embossment," on the certificate. Or the Notary can write a brief description of the document on the certificate: for example, "This certificate is attached to a _____ (title or type of document), dated _____, of _____ (number) pages, also signed by _____ (name[s] of other signer[s])."

While fraud-deterrent steps such as these can make it much more difficult for a loose certificate to be removed and misused, there is no protection against its removal and misuse. Notaries absolutely must ensure that while a certificate remains in their control, it is attached only to its intended document. A Notary never gives or mails a signed and sealed notarial certificate to another person, trusting that person to attach it to a particular document. This would be an all but indefensible action in a civil court of law.

Do Not Pre-Sign/Seal Certificates. A Notary should *never* sign and/or seal certificates ahead of time or permit other persons to attach loose notarial certificates to documents. Nor should the Notary send an unattached, signed and sealed, loose certificate through the mail, even if requested to do so by a signer who previously appeared before the Notary. These actions may facilitate fraud or forgery, and they could subject the Notary to lawsuits to recover damages resulting from the Notary's neglect or misconduct.

Selecting Certificates. It is not the role of the Notary to decide what type of certificate — thus, what type of notarization — a document needs. As ministerial officials, Notaries generally follow instructions and fill out forms that have been provided for them; they do not issue instructions and decide which forms are appropriate in a given case.

If a document is presented to a Notary without certificate wording, and if the signer doesn't know what type of notarization is appropriate, the signer should be asked to find out what kind of notarization and certificate are needed. Usually, the agency that issued the document, or the one accepting the document, can provide this information. Selecting certificates may be an unauthorized practice of law.

False Certificates. A Notary who knowingly completes a false notarial certificate may be subject to criminal penalties. A Notary would be completing a false certificate, for example, if he or she signed and sealed an acknowledgment certificate indicating a signer personally appeared when the signer actually did not.

Notaries are often pressured by employers, clients, friends, or relatives to be untruthful in their official certificates. An employer may ask the Notary to notarize a spouse's signature without the spouse being present; a client may ask the Notary to take an acknowledgment over the phone; a friend or relative may ask the Notary to consider a stranger as personally known. In complying with these requests, the Notary would have to fill out a false certificate, which is a criminal act.

If convicted of a crime of dishonesty, a New Jersey Notary may lose his or her Notary commission or be denied any future commission. The Notary may also be subject to a civil lawsuit and damages brought by the injured party. (NJSA 52:7-20, 52:7-21)

Notary Seal

Optional. New Jersey law does not require Notaries to use seals of office, but statutes *do* stipulate that a Notary must print, type, or stamp, in addition to his or her official signature, an impression of the Notary's name, preferably photocopiable. State law does specify that a seal is *not* required to validate oaths, affirmations, or affidavits. (NJSA 41:1-7, 52:7-19)

Many Notaries elect to use an inking or embossing seal to impart an appropriate sense of ceremony to their official acts. Another very practical reason for using a Notary seal on notarized documents sent to other states and nations: The absence of a seal may delay or, on occasion in foreign nations, prevent the document's acceptance.

Embossing and Inking Seals. There are two types of Notary seal: the traditional metal embosser which crimps its impression onto a paper surface; and the more modern inking stamp, usually with a rubber face, which imprints a photocopiable impression on the paper. (Many New Jersey Notaries use rubber stamps to affix their name, commission expiration date and certain other required information. See "Required Information," below.)

In many states, county recording officials prefer inking seals because they considerably simplify the process of microfilming property deeds and other recordable documents. Recorders have to smudge seal embossments with carbon or other photocopiable substances before they can be microfilmed.

Required Information. On every notarial certificate, a Notary must print, type, or stamp an impression of the Notary's name, preferably photocopiable, in order for the State Treasurer to read the name clearly. (NJSA 52:7-19)

The Notary may impress this information by using an inking seal. The National Notary Association recommends that the Notary also include the words "Notary Public," the commission expiration date, and any other pertinent information — perhaps the name of the county in which the Notary has filed his or her oath of office — in the seal.

Placement of Seal Impression. The Notary's seal impression should be placed near the Notary's signature on the notarial certificate. Whenever possible — and especially with documents that will be submitted to a public recorder — the Notary should avoid affixing the seal over any text on the document or certificate, especially if the information in the seal will be obscured. Some recorders will reject documents if writing or document text intrudes within the borders of the Notary's seal.

If there is no room for a seal, the Notary may complete and attach a loose certificate that duplicates the notarial wording on the document.

With documents that will *not* be publicly recorded, however, the recipient may allow the Notary to affix the seal over boilerplate text — the standard preprinted clauses or sections — as long as the wording within the seal is not obscured.

L.S. The letters "L.S." — from the Latin *locus sigilli*, meaning "location of the seal" — appear on many notarial certificates to indicate where the Notary seal should be placed. Only an embosser seal should be placed *over* these letters. The inking seal should be placed *near*, but not over, the letters.

Fees for Notarial Services

Maximum Fees. The following maximum fees for performing notarial acts are allowed by New Jersey law: (NJSA 22A:4-13, 22A:4-14)

- <u>Acknowledgments — $2.50</u>. For taking an acknowledgment, the fee is not to exceed $2.50 per signature.

- <u>Oaths and Affirmations — $2.50</u>. For administering an oath or affirmation or taking an affidavit, with or without a jurat certificate, the fee is not to exceed $2.50 per person or signer.

• <u>Jurats — $2.50</u>. For executing a jurat with an oath or affirmation, the fee is not to exceed the fee allowed for an oath or affidavit, $2.50.

• <u>Proof of Execution by Subscribing Witness — $2.50</u>. For taking a proof of execution by subscribing witness on a deed, the maximum fee is the same as for an acknowledgment, $2.50 per principal signer.

• <u>Real Estate Transfer</u>. In performing any of the above notarizations for a real estate transfer, regardless of the number of notarizations performed in the transaction, a Notary may charge $15.

• <u>Financing of Real Estate</u>. In performing notarizations for mortgagors in the financing of a real estate transaction, regardless of the number of notarizations performed in the transaction, a Notary may charge $25.

• <u>Protests — $2</u>. For executing a protest, the fee shall not exceed $2. For serving each additional note of protest delivered in person or by mail, in addition to the cost of postage, the fee shall not exceed $.10.

<u>Travel Fees</u>. Charges for travel by a Notary are not specified by law. Such fees are allowed only if Notary and signer agree beforehand on the amount to be charged. The signer must understand that a travel fee is not stipulated in law and is separate from the notarial fees described above.

<u>Option Not to Charge</u>. Notaries are not required to charge for their notarial services, and they may charge any fee less than the maximum. It is important, however, that the Notary maintain a consistent charging policy to prevent charges of discrimination.

<u>Overcharging</u>. Charging more than the legally

prescribed fees in executing a protest, a court may demand a Notary pay $25 for each violation to the person overcharged. (NJSA 22A:4-13)

Although the laws only prescribe penalties for protests, charging more than the maximum statutory fee for any notarial act may subject the Notary to penalties or charges of discrimination.

Blank or Incomplete Documents

Do Not Notarize. While New Jersey law does not specifically address notarizing a blank or incomplete document, this is a dangerous, unbusinesslike practice and a breach of common sense, similar to signing a blank check.

A fraudulent document could readily be created above a Notary's signed and sealed certificate on an otherwise blank paper. And, with documents containing blanks to be filled in after the notarization by a person other than the signer, there is a danger that the information inserted will be contrary to the wishes of the signer.

Any blanks in a document should be filled in by the signer *prior to* notarization. If the blanks are inapplicable and intended to be left unfilled, the signer should be asked to line through each space (using ink) or write "Not Applicable" or "N/A."

False Documents

Notary Not Responsible. It is not the duty of the Notary to verify the truthfulness or accuracy of the facts in the text of a document. In fact, Notaries are not even required to read the documents they notarize. The Notary is entitled, though, to quickly scan the instrument to extract important particulars (its title, date, and number of pages, for example) to record in an official notarial journal.

However, if a Notary happens to discover a document is false or fraudulent, the Notary — as a responsible public official — has a duty to refuse the notarization and to report the attempted fraud to appropriate authorities.

Disqualifying Interest

Impartiality. Notaries are appointed by the state to be impartial, disinterested witnesses whose screening duties help ensure the integrity of important legal and commercial transactions. Lack of impartiality by a Notary throws doubt on the integrity and lawfulness of any transaction. A Notary should never notarize his or her own signature, or notarize a transaction to which the Notary is a party or in which the Notary has any financial or beneficial interest.

Financial or Beneficial Interest. A financial or beneficial interest exists when the Notary is individually named as a principal in a financial transaction or when the Notary receives an advantage, right, privilege, property, or fee valued in excess of the lawfully prescribed notarial fee.

In regard to real estate transactions, a Notary usually is considered to have a disqualifying financial or beneficial interest when that Notary is a grantor or grantee, a mortgagor or mortgagee, a trustor or trustee, a vendor or vendee, a lessor or lessee, or a beneficiary in any way of the transaction.

Corporations. A New Jersey Notary who is a stockholder, director, officer, employee, or agent of a bank or other corporation may administer an oath to any other stockholder, director, officer, employee, or agent of the corporation. (NJSA 41:2-3)

Relatives. State officials strongly discourage Notaries from notarizing for persons related by blood or marriage because of the likelihood of a financial or beneficial interest, whether large or small and whether at the time of the transaction or in the future.

Often, a Notary will have a clear-cut disqualifying financial or beneficial interest in notarizing for a close friend or relative, especially for the Notary's spouse. If the Notary's spouse, for example, purchases a home in which the couple will live, then the Notary should not notarize the deed for the purchase.

It is often difficult for a Notary to retain impartiality with a close relative. Anyone, for example, is entitled to counsel a brother, a spouse, or other relative to sign or not to sign an important document, but such counseling is entirely inappropriate for the impartial Notary.

Refusal of Services

Legal Requests for Services. Notaries must honor all lawful and reasonable requests to notarize. In addition, a person's race, color, religion, nationality, gender or political views are not considered due cause for refusing to perform a notarial act.

Noncustomer Discrimination Discouraged. A Notary who is employed by a private employer should not discriminate between customers and noncustomers. Fees and services provided should be the same for all, whether or not the individual is a client or customer of the employer.

That said, New Jersey law does have a new provision which allows a Notary employed by a financial institution to refuse to administer oaths and affirmations to any person during business hours, as long as this is the employer's consistent policy. The Notary is not legally required to adhere to these provisions, but, of course, a failure to follow any employer's directions or policies may bring certain consequences. (NJSA 41:2-3)

Penalty. Should a Notary refuse to perform a lawfully requested notarial act — other than when restricted by the Notary's employer as described above — the Notary may be subject to charges of discrimination and liable to the injured party for any damages.

Exception. A Notary may refuse to notarize a document if he or she knows that the document is blatantly fraudulent.

Employer/Notary Agreement

Agreement to Limit Notary's Services. A Notary Public employed by a financial institution may agree to follow the employer's direction or policy to not administer oaths except in the course of business. The restriction is limited to the Notary's service during regular business hours and is valid only if the Notary agrees to the policy.

A "financial institution" is specifically defined as a state or federally chartered bank, savings bank, savings and loan association, or credit union. (NJSA 41:2-3)

It may be helpful to the Notary to have the agreement in writing to prevent any haggling when limiting these services. If challenged, the written agreement may serve to identify the employer's consistent policy, perhaps protecting the Notary and the employer from charges of discrimination.

Reasonable Care

Responsibility. As public servants, Notaries must act responsibly and exercise reasonable care in the performance of their official duties. If a Notary fails to do so, he or she may be subject to a civil suit to recover financial damages caused by the Notary's error or omission.

In general, reasonable care is a degree of concern and attentiveness that a person of normal intelligence and responsibility would exhibit. If a Notary can show a judge or jury that he or she did everything expected of a reasonable person, the judge or jury may be required by law to find the Notary blameless and not liable for damages.

Complying with all pertinent laws is the first rule of reasonable care for a Notary. And, if there are no statutory guidelines in a given instance, the Notary should go to extremes to use common sense and prudence. (See "Steps to Proper Notarization," pages 16–20.)

Notarial Records. Although not required by law, a Notary's best proof of having exercised reasonable care is a detailed, accurate journal of notarial acts. Such entries as the serial numbers of ID cards and the signatures of credible identifying witnesses can show that the Notary took steps to positively identify every signer. Possession by the Notary of a well-maintained recordbook can prevent lawsuits that falsely claim the Notary was negligent.

Unauthorized Practice of Law

Do Not Assist in Legal Matters. A nonattorney Notary may not give legal advice or accept fees for legal advice. As a ministerial official, the nonattorney Notary generally is not permitted to assist a signer in drafting, preparing, selecting, completing, or understanding a document or transaction. A Notary is only responsible for the information on his or her notarial certificate.

The Notary should not fill in the blank spaces in the text of a document for other persons, tell others what documents they need or how to draft them, nor advise others about the legal sufficiency of a document — and especially not for a fee.

A Notary, of course, may fill in the blanks on the portion of any document containing the notarial certificate. And a Notary, as a private individual, may prepare legal documents that he or she is personally a party to, but the Notary may not notarize his or her own signature on these same documents.

Do Not Determine Notarial Act. A Notary who is not an attorney may not determine the type of notarial act to perform or decide which type of notarial certificate to attach. This is beyond the scope of the Notary's expertise and might be considered the unauthorized practice of law. The Notary should only follow instructions provided by the document, its signer, its issuing or receiving agency, or an attorney.

If a document lacks notarial certificate wording, the Notary must ask the document signer what type of notarization — acknowledgment or jurat — is required. The Notary may then type the appropriate notarial wording on the document or attach a preprinted, loose certificate. If the signer does not know what type of notarization is required, the issuing or receiving agency should be contacted. This decision is *never* to be made by the Notary, unless the Notary is also an attorney.

Exceptions. Specially trained, nonattorney Notaries certified or licensed in a particular field (e.g., real estate, insurance, escrow, etc.) may offer advice or prepare documents related to that field only. Paralegals under the supervision of an attorney may give advice about documents in routine legal matters.

Signature by Mark
Mark Serves as Signature. A person who cannot sign

his or her name because of illiteracy or a physical disability may instead use a mark — an "X", for example — as a signature. (NJSA 46:14-4.2)

<u>Witnesses</u>. For a signature by mark to be notarized, the National Notary Association recommends that there be two witnesses to the making of the mark *in addition* to the Notary.

Both witnesses should sign the document and the Notary's journal. One witness should legibly print the marker's name beside the mark on the document. It is recommended that a mark also be affixed in the Notary's journal.

<u>Notarization Procedures</u>. Because a properly witnessed mark is considered a signature under custom and law, no special notarial certificate is required. As required with any other signer, the marker must be positively identified.

Notarizing for Minors

<u>Persons Under Age 18</u>. Generally, individuals must reach the age of majority before they can handle their own legal affairs and sign documents for themselves. In New Jersey, the age of majority is 18. Normally, parents or court-appointed guardians will sign on a minor's behalf. In certain cases, where minors are engaged in business transactions or serving as witnesses in court, they may lawfully sign documents and have their signatures notarized.

<u>Include Age Next to Signature</u>. When notarizing for a minor, the Notary should ask the young signer to write his or her age next to the signature to alert any person relying on the document that the signer is a minor. The Notary is not required to verify the minor signer's age.

<u>Identification</u>. The method for identifying a minor is the same as that for an adult. However, determining the identity of a minor can be a problem, because minors often do not possess acceptable identification documents such as driver's licenses or passports. If the minor does not have an acceptable ID, then the other methods of

identifying acknowledgers must be used, either the Notary's personal knowledge of the minor or the oath of a credible identifying witness who can identify the minor. (See "Credible Identifying Witness(es)," pages 45–46.)

Authentication

Documents Sent Out of State. Documents notarized in New Jersey and sent to other states may be required by the entity receiving the document to bear written proof that the Notary's signature and seal (if used) are genuine and that the Notary had authority to act at the time of notarization. This process of proving the genuineness of an official signature and seal is called *authentication* or *legalization*.

In New Jersey, the proof is in the form of an authenticating certificate attached to the notarized document by either the county clerk's office where the Notary's signature and certificate of official character are filed, or the New Jersey State Treasurer's office.

The county clerk is restricted to providing authentication certificates only to Notaries residing — or working, in the case of nonresidents — in their counties, or to Notaries who have filed copies of their Commission and Qualification Certificates in their counties. The State Treasurer is authorized to issue authenticating certificates relating to *any* Notary in the state, regardless of where the Notary has filed the Commission or Qualification Certificates. (NJSA 52:7-15, 52:7-16)

Authentication certificates are known by different names: certificates of authority, certificates of capacity, certificates of authenticity, certificates of prothonotary, and "flags."

Procedure. It is not the Notary's responsibility to request an authenticating certificate for a signer's notarized document. The individual seeking to obtain an authentication certificate must include a cover letter indicating the quantity of documents requiring authentication, along with the notarized documents, and the name, address, and telephone number of the person making the request. The request should be sent to either the clerk of the county in which the Notary has filed the

Notary Commission or duplicate Qualification Certificates (see "County Clerks' Offices," pages 104–105), or one of the Secretary of State offices at:

Address:
Department of Treasury
Division of Revenue
Notary Public Unit
P.O. Box 452,
Trenton, NJ 08625
Telephone: (609) 633-8257

In Person, Go to:
State of New Jersey
Notary Public Section
225 West State Street
Trenton, NJ 08608-1001

Fees. The State Treasurer charges $25 per document for service via mail ($5 for documents relating to an adoption). Expedited service is available for an addition $15 per document. Payment should be made by check or money order payable to the "Treasurer, State of New Jersey." If requesting authentication from a county, the individual should contact the county clerk for the fee in the particular county (see "County Clerks' Offices," pages 104–105).

Documents Sent Out of Country. If the notarized document is going out of the United States, a chain authentication process may be necessary. Additional certificates of authority may have to be obtained from the U.S. Department of State in Washington, D.C., a foreign consulate in Washington, D.C. and a ministry of foreign affairs in the particular foreign nation.

Apostilles and the Hague Convention. More than 80 nations, including the United States, subscribe to a treaty under auspices of the Hague Conference that simplifies authentication of notarized documents exchanged between any of these nations. The official name of this treaty, adopted by the Conference on October 5, 1961, is the Hague Convention Abolishing the Requirement of Legalization for Foreign Public Documents. (For a list of the subscribing countries, see "Hague Convention Nations," pages 111–113.)

Under this Hague Convention, only one authenticating certificate called an *apostille* is necessary to ensure acceptance in these subscribing countries. (*Apostille* is French for "notation".) It is not necessary to obtain an authentication certificate from the county prior to requesting an *apostille*.

In New Jersey, *apostilles* are issued by the State Treasurer's office (described above) for a fee of $25 per document for service via mail, or $35 per document for expedited service. *Apostilles* are not available from the county clerk.

An *apostille* must be specifically requested in writing, including the name, address, and telephone number of the person making the request. The letter also must identify the nation to which the document will be sent. The person requesting the apostille must send the letter, the notarized document, and the appropriate fee to one of the State Treasurer offices listed on page 64.

It should be noted that it is *not* the Notary's responsibility to obtain an *apostille*, but rather, it is the responsibility of the party sending the document out of the country.

Advertising

False or Misleading Advertising. A Notary's commission may be revoked or suspended if the Notary advertises or claims to have powers not authorized by law. For example, a Notary may not claim to have authority to officially certify the translation of a document, since this is not a power given by New Jersey law.

For practicing fraud or deceit in advertising or in any other activity as a Notary, the Notary may be found guilty of a crime of the second degree or above. (NJSA 57:7-20, 57:7-21)

Foreign Languages

Foreign-Language Documents. While New Jersey law

does not directly address the notarization of documents written in a language other than English, it does set restrictions on the recording of non-English documents.

Any document conveying title to real estate that is presented for recording in a county office must be completely in English, including the Notary's certificate and any authenticating certificates. (Proper names may be in a foreign language, as long as the letters used are those of the English language.) A non-English-language conveyance may only be recorded if accompanied by a duly certified English-language translation. (NJSA 46:15-1.1)

Although it is not expressly illegal to notarize a document written in a language the Notary cannot understand, there are difficulties and dangers in doing so. The foremost danger is that the document may have been misrepresented to the Notary. Ideally, documents in foreign languages should be referred to Notaries who read these languages; in large cities, such multilingual Notaries are often found in ethnic neighborhoods or in foreign consulates.

If a Notary chooses to notarize a document that he or she cannot read, at the very least, the notarial certificate should be in English or in a language the Notary can read, and the signature notarized should be written in characters that the Notary is familiar with.

Foreign-Speaking Signers. There should always be direct communication between the Notary and document signer — whether in English or any other language. The Notary should never rely on an intermediary or interpreter to determine a signer's willingness or competence. A third party may have a motive for misrepresenting the circumstances to the Notary and/or to the signer.

Immigration

Do Not Give Advice. Nonattorney Notaries may never advise others on the subject of immigration, nor help others prepare immigration documents — and especially not for a fee. Notaries who offer immigration advice to others may be subject to penalties for the unauthorized practice of law.

Documents. Certain immigration documents may be notarized, including Form I-134/I-864, also known as the "Affidavit of Support." However, federal law does pose certain restrictions on the Notary in the area of immigration. (See "Naturalization Certificates," below.)

Naturalization Certificates. A Notary may be in violation of federal law if he or she makes a typewritten, photostatic, or any other type of copy of a certificate of naturalization or notarizes it. Severe penalties are prescribed, including imprisonment.

Military Officer Notarizations

May Notarize Worldwide. Certain U.S. military officers may notarize for military personnel and their dependents anywhere in the world. Under federal statutory authority, the following persons are authorized to act as Notaries:

• Civilian attorneys employed as legal assistance attorneys and licensed to practice law in the United States.

• Judge advocates on active duty or training as reservists on inactive duty.

• All adjutants, assistant adjutants, acting adjutants and personnel adjutants.

• Enlisted paralegals, personnel rank E-4 or higher, on active duty or training on inactive duty.

• Active duty personnel who are commissioned officers or senior noncommissioned officers (rank E-7 or higher) who are stationed at a Geographically Separated Unit (GSU) or location where no authorized Notary official is available, and who are appointed in writing by the unit's servicing general court-martial convening authority.

Certificate. When signing documents in their official capacity, military-officer Notaries must specify the date and location of the notarization, their title and office, and cite Title 10 U.S.C. 1044a. (U.S. Code, Title 10, Sections 936, 1044a)

Authentication. Authentication of a military-officer notarization certificate is typically not required.

Wills

Do Not Offer Advice. A Notary risks prosecution for the unauthorized practice of law in advising a signer how to proceed with a will. In addition, the Notary's ill-informed advice may adversely affect the affairs of the signer. The format of a will is dictated by strict laws of each state, and any deviation may result in nullification. In some cases, holographic (handwritten) wills have actually been voided by notarization.

A Notary should notarize a document described as a will *only* if a notarial certificate is provided or stipulated for each signer, and the signers are not asking questions about how to proceed. Any such questions should be answered by an attorney.

Living Wills. Documents popularly called "living wills" may be notarized. These are not actual wills, but written statements of a signer's wishes concerning medical treatment in the event he or she is unable to issue instructions on his or her own behalf.

Self-Proved Wills. In New Jersey, self-proving wills may require the signatures of the testator and two witnesses to be notarized. (NJSA 3B:3-5, 3B:3-7, 3B:3-8)

Certificate for Self-Proved Will. The notarial certificate for a self-proved will must be in substantially the following form: (NJSA 3B:3-5)

State of New Jersey)
) ss.
County of _____)

We, _____, the testator and the witnesses, respectively,

whose names are signed to the attached or foregoing instrument, being duly sworn, do hereby declare to the undersigned authority that the testator signed and executed the instrument as his/her last will and that he/she had signed willingly (or willingly directed another to sign for him/her), and that he/she executed it as his/her free and voluntary act for the purposes therein expressed, and that each of the witnesses, in the presence and hearing of the testator, signed the will as witness and that to the best of his/her knowledge the testator was at that time 18 years of age or older, of sound mind and under no constraint or undue influence.

Testator _____
Witness _____
Witness _____

Subscribed, sworn to and acknowledged before me by _____, the testator, and subscribed and sworn to before me by _____ and _____, witnesses, this _____ day of _____ (month and year).

_____ (Signed)   (Notary's Seal)
_____ (Official capacity of officer)

Advance Directives for Health Care

<u>Purpose</u>. Any individual may execute an advance directive for health care. The directive must be signed and dated in the presence of two witnesses or acknowledged before a Notary Public. (NJSA 26:2H-56)

<u>Witnesses</u>. For an advance directive, there may be two witnesses, other than a health care representative, to witness the signing of the directive by the individual (declarant). Each of the witnesses must sign the document and also take an oath (or affirmation) to attest that the declarant appeared to be of sound mind and not under any undue influence or emotional duress. (NJSA 26:2H-56)

<u>Revocation, Suspension, or Change in Directive</u>. At any time, a declarant may modify, revoke, or suspend an advanced directive by communicating to any person, including a health care representative, the desire to change his or her directive. (NJSA 26:2H-57)

Digital Signatures

No Notarization Procedures Established. Notaries should *not* attempt to notarize digital signatures. As yet, there are no statutory procedures in New Jersey for doing so.

Weddings

Cannot Perform Ceremony. New Jersey Notaries have no authority to solemnize nuptials, unless they are also religious officials. Even so, the marriage would be performed only in the capacity of religious official, not as a Notary Public. This means that, among other things, the Notary may not attest to the performance of a marriage using the title "Notary Public."

Only Notaries in Maine, South Carolina, and Florida are empowered to perform marriages strictly by virtue of holding a notarial commission.

MISCONDUCT, FINES, AND PENALTIES

Misconduct

General Prohibitions. Although New Jersey statute sets out very little to define what may be construed as official misconduct, the on-line edition of the New Jersey Notary Public Manual defines some general acts that are prohibited.

A New Jersey Notary should never:

• Pre-date a certificate prior to the date of execution of the document;

• Share with another person a journal, seal, or other personalized Notary equipment;

• Prepare or draft legal documents or offer legal advice or advice on matters pertaining to land titles;

• Represent another person in a legal proceeding, especially in the capacity of a Notary; or

• Collect delinquent bills or claims for others, especially in the capacity of a Notary.

Application Misstatement. As stated on the Notary commission application materials, substantial and material misstatement or omission of information on the application for a Notary commission may be reason for the State Treasurer to reject the application.

Failure to File Oath of Office. A Notary Public must file his or her oath of office within three months after the date specified on the Notary Public Commission Certificate. Failure to file within this time limit may result in cancellation or revocation of the appointment. (NJSA 52:7-14)

Criminal Conviction. Conviction in New Jersey or any other state for a crime or any offense involving dishonesty — such as fraud or misrepresentation — or of a crime of the first or second degree may be reason for the State Treasurer to refuse to grant a Notary's commission. (NJSA 52:7-20, 52:7-21)

Falsely Acting as a Notary. Any person who is not a Notary and who represents himself or herself as a Notary Public or any other public officer is guilty of a "disorderly persons offense" and may be ordered to pay a fine not to exceed $1000, to make restitution for monetary damages, or both. (NJSA 2C:28-8, 2C:43-3)

Failure of Duty. Failure to fully and faithfully discharge the duties or responsibilities of a Notary — such as failing to complete a Notarial certificate — may subject the Notary to charges of misconduct and removal from office.

Failure to Affix Name. On every notarial certificate, the Notary must affix, in addition to his or her official signature, his or her name by printing, typing, or impressing the name by seal or mechanical stamp. (NJSA 52:7-19)
Failure to include the required information may cause a document to be rejected and may subject a Notary to lawsuits by injured parties.

Advertising Practices
False or Misleading Advertising. The use of dishonest, false or misleading advertising by a Notary to represent that he or she has duties, rights and privileges not given by law may be reason for the State Treasurer to take action against the Notary's commission.

Translating "Notary Public" into Spanish. Because Latin Notaries often have powers similar to that of attorneys, Notaries are generally discouraged from translating the term "Notary Public" into the Spanish *Notario Publico* or *Notaria Publica*. Notaries who do so may be accused of illegal advertising practices and subject to removal from office.

Immigration
Immigration Advice. A nonattorney Notary may not claim to be an immigration expert or counselor, nor help others prepare immigration documents. Such actions may be construed as an unauthorized practice of law and may result in the revocation of the Notary's commission.

Naturalization Certificate Copies or Notarizations. A Notary may be in violation of federal law if he or she makes a typewritten, photostatic, or any other copy of a certificate of naturalization or notarizes it.

Notarial Acts
Notarizing Own Signature. The New Jersey State Treasurer has said that Notaries are not permitted to notarize their own signatures. If done, the Notary may risk being charged with having a disqualifying interest in the notarization.

Overcharging. A Notary who charges more than the legally prescribed fees for executing a protest is subject to civil action in which the person overcharged may seek to recover $25 plus court costs. (NJSA 22A:4-13)
Although the laws only prescribe penalties for protests, a Notary who charges more than the maximum statutory fee for any notarial act may subject to charges of discrimination.

A New Jersey commissioner of deeds who charges greater fees than allowed by law is subject to removal by the Governor. (NJSA 56:6-13)

<u>False Acknowledgments</u>. A Notary must ensure that a certificate for an acknowledgment reflects the date the signer actually appeared before the Notary. A certificate that indicates a different date than when the signer actually appeared is considered to be fraudulent.

<u>False Certificate</u>. A Notary who knowingly completes a false certificate may be subject to criminal penalties.

<u>Telephone Acknowledgments</u>. New Jersey law expressly requires document signers to personally appear before the Notary at the time of notarization. Telephone notarizations are *not* permitted. (NJSA 46:14-2.1)

<u>Dishonesty or Fraud</u>. Performance of a notarial act involving dishonesty — such as fraud or misrepresentation — or of a crime of the first or second degree may be reason for the State Treasurer to refuse to grant a Notary's commission. (NJSA 52:7-20, 52:7-21)

<u>Undue Influence</u>. Since Notaries are appointed to serve as impartial witnesses, a Notary must never attempt to influence a person to execute or not to execute a document or transaction requiring a notarial act.

Unauthorized Practice of Law
<u>Never Give Advice</u>. Giving advice about a legal document when one is not a lawyer may be construed as the unauthorized practice of law and may be reason for the State Treasurer to take action against a Notary's commission.

In addition to penalties imposed by the State Treasurer, the Supreme Court has the power to prosecute for criminal contempt any person who unlawfully practices or assumes to practice law.

Nonattorney Notaries cannot give counsel or advice on the drawing of agreements, the organization of corporations. They cannot prepare such papers or draft legal documents of any kind.

Civil Lawsuit

Liability for Damages. A Notary may be subject to removal from office, or civil or criminal legal actions, for willful violations, including fraud and dishonesty.

In addition, if convicted of a crime involving dishonesty or of a crime in the first or second degree, the Notary will be subject to removal from office or denial of appointment when applying for a subsequent commission. (NJSA 52:7-20, 52:7-21)

Found Liable for Fraud or Misrepresentation. Being found liable for damages in a suit accusing fraud, misrepresentation, or violation of state laws may be reason for the State Treasurer to take action against a Notary's commission. A Notary found guilty of such misconduct or negligence may be subject to a civil lawsuit to recover damages. (NJSA 52:7-21)

Right to Respond to Charges

Filing a Complaint. Should an individual wish to file a complaint against a Notary, the complaint should be in writing and directed to: Notary Public Section, P.O. Box 452, Trenton, New Jersey 08625.

Administrative Action Against Notary. Before the State Treasurer takes action against a commission, the accused Notary usually has a chance to respond to the charges. If there is no response from the accused Notary, the State Treasurer will take appropriate action. ∎

Test Your Knowledge

Trial Exam

Instructions. This examination is designed to test your knowledge of the basic concepts of notarization based on general principles and the notarial practices and procedures in New Jersey. Although the state of New Jersey does not require prospective Notaries to pass an exam before granting a commission, Notaries should thoroughly study this *Primer* and the pertinent New Jersey statutes to become familiar with notarial acts and duties.

Work through this exam without looking at the answers, then check your responses and note where you need additional study. Careful review of "Notary Laws Explained" (pages 21–74), the reprinted New Jersey Notary statutes (pages 81–102), "10 Most-Asked Questions" (pages 10–15) and "Steps to Proper Notarization" (pages 16–20) will produce the answers.

A perfect score on this examination is 100 points. There are:

- 20 true/false questions worth 1 point each.
- 5 multiple-choice questions worth 4 points each.
- 5 fill-in-the-blank questions worth 4 points each.
- 5 essay questions worth 8 points each.

Now, get a separate sheet of paper and a pen or pencil, and get ready to test your knowledge.

Part 1: True/False. For the following statements, answer true or false. Each correct answer is worth 1 point:

1. Notaries may act only in the county where they are commissioned. True or false?

2. The maximum Notary fee for taking an acknowledgment is $2. True or false?

3. Oaths and affirmations have the same legal effect. True or false?

4. Protests are one of the most common forms of notarization. True or false?

5. Notaries are obligated to ensure the truthfulness of the statements in the documents they notarize. True or false?

6. It is the duty of the Notary to decide what type of notarization is appropriate for a given document. True or false?

7. Though not legally required in New Jersey, use of a Notary seal and journal is a good practice. True or false?

8. A subscribing witness must sign the document in addition to the principal signer. True or false?

9. An employee of a corporation may administer oaths to other officers and stockholders of that corporation. True or false?

10. Notaries may use their own wills as models in advising clients about how to handle their estates. True or false?

11. An affidavit must be signed in the Notary's presence. True or false?

12. An acknowledged document, such as a deed, must always be signed in the Notary's presence. True or false?

13. A Social Security card and a birth certificate offer reliable proof of a document signer's identity. True or false?

14. An affiant must do more than merely nod in assent to an affirmation. True or false?

15. The letters "S.S." indicate that Notaries must write in their Social Security numbers. True or false?

16. Certifying a copy is not an official notarial act in New Jersey. True or false?

17. It is ill-advised to notarize a document whose blank spaces will be filled in later. True or false?

18. On a notarial certificate, the venue indicates where the Notary's oath has been filed. True or false?

19. Although technically different, the terms "affiant" and "deponent" are sometimes interchanged.
True or false?

20. Notaries employed by financial institutions may limit certain services to customers only. True or false?

Multiple Choice. Choose the one best answer to each question. Each correct answer is worth 4 points.

1. When executing an acknowledgment, a Notary certifies that ...
    a. the signer took an oath or affirmation.
    b. the signer was positively identified by the Notary.
    c. the signer signed the Notary's journal.

2. In executing a jurat, a Notary certifies that ...
    a. the signer acknowledged his or her signature.
    b. the signer signed in the Notary's presence.
    c. the signer has no direct interest in the document.

3. Non-English-language real property deeds ...
    a. cannot be notarized in New Jersey.
    b. are illegal in New Jersey.
    c. cannot be recorded in the state of New Jersey without a translation.

4. Notaries may be liable …
    a. only for their intentional acts.
    b. only for damages suffered by the signer.
    c. for all damages caused by their misconduct.

5. It could be the unauthorized practice of law to …
    a. explain a paragraph in an immigration document to the signer.
    b. provide a notarial certificate requested by the signer.
    c. type a paper following the signer's instructions.

<u>Fill in the Blank</u>. Write in the word or phrase that best completes each sentence. Each correct answer is worth 4 points.

1. A _____ must sometimes be attached to a notarized document sent out of state.

2. An affirmation is a solemn, spoken pledge that does not refer to a _____.

3. The best identification cards contain the following three elements:
a) _____; b) _____; and c) _____.

4. Without ID cards or personal knowledge of a signer's identity, Notaries may rely on the oath of a _____ to identify the stranger.

5. The state official who appoints and regulates Notaries is the _____.

<u>Essay</u>. Reply to each question or statement with a short paragraph. Each complete and correct response is worth 8 points.

1. Under what conditions should a Notary execute a protest?

2. How does a proof of execution by subscribing witness work?

3. What is an *apostille* and when is it used?

4. Why should a Notary always complete the journal entry before filling out a notarial certificate?

5. Outline the differences between an acknowledgment certificate and a jurat.

Test Answers

True/False. 1. F; 2. F; 3. T; 4. F; 5. F; 6. F; 7. T; 8. T; 9. T; 10. F; 11. T; 12. F; 13. F; 14. T; 15. F; 16. T; 17. T; 18. F; 19. T; 20. T

Multiple Choice. 1. b; 2. b; 3. c; 4. c; 5. a

Fill In The Blank. 1. Certificate of Authentication; 2. Supreme Being; 3. Photograph, signature, and physical description; 4. Credible identifying witness; 5. State Treasurer.

Essay. Responses should include the basic information in the paragraphs below:

1. Since protests are complicated notarial acts, Notaries should only execute them if they understand the legal and financial terminology used in the protest certificate, or if they are under the supervision of a person with such an understanding. (See pages 41–43.)

2. A proof of execution in lieu of an acknowledgment is sometimes used when a document's principal signer is unavailable to appear before a Notary. In most such cases, the principal will be out of town, out of state or even out of the country. A so-called subscribing witness who has either seen the principal sign the document or taken the principal's acknowledgment of the signature may present this document to a Notary on the principal's behalf. The witness must sign ("subscribe") the document in addition to the principal. The witness, who should be personally known to the Notary, is given an oath by the Notary. A person who is a grantee or beneficiary of a document should not serve as a subscribing witness. (See pages 39–41.)

3. An *apostille* is a certificate authenticating the signature and seal of a Notary that is issued under provisions of an international treaty, signed by more than 50 nations, called the Hague Convention Abolishing the Requirement of Legalization for Foreign Public Documents. For notarized documents exchanged between the subscribing nations, this treaty streamlines the time-consuming authentication process known as "chain certification" by requiring only one authenticating certificate, the *apostille* (French for "notation"). *Apostilles* for New Jersey Notaries are issued by the State Treasurer. (See pages 63–65.)

4. Filling out a journal entry before completing a notarial certificate prevents a signer from taking the document and leaving before an important record of the notarization is made in the journal. (See pages 48–50.)

5. An acknowledgment certificate certifies that the signer of the document personally appeared before the Notary on the date and in the county indicated. It also certifies that the signer's identity was satisfactorily proven to the Notary and that the signer acknowledged having signed freely. A jurat certifies that the person signing the document did so in the Notary's presence, that the person appeared before the Notary on the date and in the county indicated, that the person was also positively identified, and that the Notary administered an oath or affirmation to the signer. (See pages 30–32 and 36–37.)

Tally Your Score

After checking your answers, add up your score. Then look at the grading scale below to determine how you stand:

- 90–100:   Excellent!
- 80–89:   Good, but some review needed.
- 70–79:   Fair. Reread the parts of the *Primer* covering the answers you missed.
- Below 70:   Below par. Study the laws thoroughly again. ■

New Jersey Laws Pertaining to Notaries Public

Reprinted on the following pages are pertinent sections of the New Jersey Statutes Annotated (NJSA) affecting Notaries and notarial acts. These statutes, along with this *Primer*, should be studied thoroughly before executing any notarial acts.

Citations at the end of each section indicate the most recent legislative action on the particular section. Three asterisks (* * *) in the text of a section indicate that irrelevant material has been omitted by the National Notary Association editors.

NOTE: Pursuant to the authority of the Executive Reorganization Act (NJSA 52:14C-1, et. seq.), all functions of the Division of Commercial Recording — which includes the Notary Public Section — have been transferred from the Secretary of State to the Department of Treasury.

NEW JERSEY STATUTES ANNOTATED

Title 52. State Government, Departments and Officers [Notary Public Act]

52:7-10. Short title
This act shall be known and may be cited as the "Notaries Public Act of 1979."
L.1979, c. 460, s. 1.

52:7-11. Notaries public
a. The Secretary of State shall appoint so many notaries public as the Secretary of State shall deem necessary to commission, who

shall hold their respective offices for the term of five years, but may be removed from office at the pleasure of the Secretary of State.

b. A person desiring to be appointed and commissioned a notary public shall make application to the Secretary of State on a form prescribed by the Secretary of State and endorsed by a member of the Legislature or the Secretary of State or Assistant Secretary of State. Renewals thereof shall be made in the same manner as the original application.

c. The fee to be collected by the Secretary of State for that appointment or renewal shall be $25.00.

L.1979, c. 460, s. 2; amended 1987, c. 435, s. 21.

52:7-12. Minimum age

No person shall be appointed a notary public unless he is 18 years of age or older.

L.1979, c. 460, s. 3.

52:7-13. Appointment of nonresidents; requirements

No person shall be denied appointment as a notary public on account of residence outside of this State, provided such person resides in a State adjoining this State and maintains, or is regularly employed in, an office in this State. Before any such nonresident shall be appointed and commissioned as a notary public, he shall file with the Secretary of State an affidavit setting forth his residence and the address of his office or place of employment in this State. Any such nonresident notary public shall file with the Secretary of State a certificate showing any change of residence or of his office or place of employment address in this State.

L.1979, c. 460, s. 4.

52:7-14. Oath; filing; certificate of commission and qualification

a. Within 3 months of the receipt of his commission, each notary public shall take and subscribe an oath before the clerk of the county in which he resides, faithfully and honestly to discharge the duties of his office, and that he will make and keep a true record of all such matters as are required by law, which oath shall be filed with said clerk. The oath of office of a nonresident notary public shall be taken and subscribed before the clerk of the county in which he maintains his office or is employed in this State.

b. Upon the administration of said oath, the said clerk shall cause the notary public to indorse a certificate of commission and qualification and shall transmit said certificate to the Secretary of State within 10 days of the administration of said oath.

c. The Secretary of State shall cancel and revoke the appointment of any notary public who fails to take and subscribe said oath within

3 months of the receipt of his commission and any appointment so canceled and revoked shall be null, void and of no effect.

L.1979, c. 460, s. 5.

52:7-15. State-wide authority; filing certificates of commission and qualification with county clerks

a. A notary public who has been duly commissioned and qualified is authorized to perform his duties throughout the State.

b. Any notary public, after having been duly commissioned and qualified, shall, upon request, receive from the clerk of the county where he has qualified, as many certificates of his commission and qualification as he shall require for filing with other county clerks of this State, and upon receipt of such certificates the notary public may present the same, together with his autograph signature, to such county clerks as he may desire, for filing.

L.1979, c. 460, s. 6.

52:7-16. County clerk to attach certificate of authority to notaries' certificates of proof, acknowledgements or affidavits

The county clerk of the county in which a notary public resides or the county clerk of any county where such notary public shall have filed his autograph signature and certificate, as provided in section 6 of this act, shall, upon request, subjoin to any certificate of proof, acknowledgement or affidavit signed by the notary public, a certificate under the clerk's hand and seal stating that the notary public was at the time of taking such proof, acknowledgement or affidavit duly commissioned and sworn and residing in this State, and was as such an officer of this State duly authorized to take and certify said proof, acknowledgement or affidavit as well as to take and certify the proof or acknowledgement of deeds for the conveyance of lands, tenements or hereditaments and other instruments in writing to be recorded in this State; that said proof, acknowledgement or affidavit is duly executed and taken according to the laws of this State; that full faith and credit are and ought to be given to the official acts of the notary public, and that the county clerk is well acquainted with the handwriting of the notary public and believes the signature to the instrument to which the certificate is attached is his genuine signature.

L.1979, c. 460, s. 7.

52:7-17. Fee

The Secretary of State shall, by regulation, fix a fee to be charged to each notary for the costs of printing and distribution to each applicant of a manual prescribing the powers, duties and responsibilities of a notary.

L.1979, c. 460, s. 8.

52:7-18. Statement by notary public after change in name; filing; evidence of continuance of powers and privileges

After a notary public adopts a name different from that which he used at the time he was commissioned, and before he signs his name to any document which he is authorized or required to sign as notary public, he shall make and sign a statement in writing and under oath, on a form prescribed and furnished by the Secretary of State, setting out the circumstances under which he has adopted the new name. The statement shall set forth whether the new name has been adopted through marriage or by a change of name proceeding or otherwise, and such other information as the Secretary of State shall require.

The statement shall be filed in the office of the Secretary of State and in the office of the clerk of the county where he qualified as a notary public and in the office of the clerk of any county in which he may have filed a certificate of his commission and qualification.

Such statement, or a certified copy thereof, shall be evidence of the right of said notary public to continue to exercise the powers and privileges and perform the duties of a notary public in his changed and new name.

L.1979, c. 460, s. 9.

52:7-19. Affixation of name

Each notary public, in addition to subscribing his autograph signature to any jurat upon the administration of any oath or the taking of any acknowledgement or proof, shall affix thereto his name in such a manner and by such means, including, but not limited to, printing, typing, or impressing by seal or mechanical stamp, as will enable the Secretary of State easily to read said name.

L.1979, c. 460, s. 10.

52:7-20. Conviction of offense involving dishonesty or crime of second degree; prohibition of appointment

No person shall be appointed a notary public if he has been convicted under the laws of this State of an offense involving dishonesty or of a crime of the second degree or above, but nothing in this section shall be deemed to supersede P.L.1968, c. 282 (C. 2A:168A-1 et seq.).

L.1981, c. 487, s. 1, eff. Jan. 12, 1982.

52:7-21. Conviction under laws of another state or United States; prohibition of appointment

No person shall be appointed a notary public if he has been convicted under the laws of another state, or of the United States, of an offense or crime involving dishonesty or which, if committed in this State, would be a crime of the second degree or above, but nothing in this section shall be deemed to supersede P.L.1968, c. 282 (C. 2A:168A-1 et seq.).

L.1981, c. 487, s. 2, eff. Jan. 12, 1982.

Title 2A. Administration of Civil and Criminal Justice

2A:82-6. Copies of record of protest as evidence

If it appears that the notary or other officer of this state by whom any bill of exchange or promissory note was protested has died or removed from the state or, after diligent inquiry, his place of residence cannot be discovered, the record deposited in the county clerk's office, as required by section 7:5-5 of the title Bills, Notes and Checks, of the Revised Statutes, or a copy thereof certified by such clerk, shall be received as competent evidence of the matter contained in such record.

When the register or other book of any notary public appointed and qualified under the laws of any state of the United States containing a record of the official acts of such notary public by him done in pursuance of his office is, in pursuance of the law of such state, by reason of the death, removal or other disability of the notary public, deposited in the office of the clerk, prothonotary or recorder of deeds of the city, town or county in which the notary public resided at the time of his acting as notary public, a copy of the record or of any part thereof respecting the protesting of any note or bill of exchange protested by the notary public, and the time when, place where and upon whom demand of acceptance or payment was made, with a copy of the notice of nonacceptance or nonpayment (if a copy of the notice shall appear on said record), how the notice of nonacceptance or nonpayment was served, and the time when, or if sent, in what manner, and the time when, and to whom, duly certified under the hand and seal of such clerk, prothonotary or recorder of deeds, or otherwise proved to be truly taken from said record, shall be held and received in all the courts of this state as competent evidence of the facts therein recited, and also of the official character of the notary public. When it shall appear from such record that the said note or bill of exchange had been protested for want of acceptance or payment thereof, and that the said notary public making such protest had duly notified the drawer or indorsers, by mail, of the demand of payment or acceptance and refusal thereof, without specifying the names or the post office address of such drawer or indorsers, the copy of the record certified or proved as aforesaid, shall be held and received in all courts of this state as competent evidence that the drawer and indorsers of such note or bill of exchange were duly notified of such demand and refusal.

2A:82-7. Certificate of protest as evidence

The certificate of a notary public of this state or of any other state of the United States, under his hand and official seal accompanying any bill of exchange or promissory note which has been protested by such notary for nonacceptance or nonpayment, shall be received in all the courts of this state as competent evidence of the official character of such notary, and also of the facts therein certified as to the presentment and dishonor of such bill or note and of the time and manner of giving or sending notice of dishonor to the parties to such bill or note.

2A:82-17. Certificates of acknowledgment or proof of instruments as evidence of execution thereof

If any instrument heretofore made and executed or hereafter to be made and executed shall have been acknowledged, by any party who shall have executed it, or the execution thereof by such party shall have been proved by one or more of the subscribing witnesses to such instrument, in the manner and before one of the officers provided and required by law for the acknowledgment or proof of instruments in order to entitle them to be recorded, and, when a certificate of such acknowledgment or proof shall be written upon or under, or be annexed to such instrument and signed by such officer in the manner prescribed by law, such certificate of acknowledgment or proof shall be and constitute prima facie evidence of the due execution of such instrument by such party. Such instrument shall be received in evidence in any court or proceeding in this state in the same manner and to the same effect as though the execution of such instrument by such party had been proved by other evidence.

2A:82-18. Certification or authentication of instruments not acknowledged or proved; effect as evidence

If any instrument heretofore made and executed or hereafter to be made and executed, although not acknowledged or proved, shall have been certified or authenticated, as to the execution thereof by any party thereto, in any manner which may be prescribed by law in order to entitle such instrument to be recorded in any public office of this state without a certificate of acknowledgment or proof thereof, such certification or authentication shall be and constitute prima facie evidence of the due execution of such instrument by such party. Such instrument shall be received in evidence in any court or proceeding in this state, in the same manner and to the same effect as though the execution of such instrument by such party had been proved by other evidence.

Title 2C. The New Jersey Code of Criminal Justice

2C:28-8. Impersonating a public servant

A person commits a disorderly persons offense if he falsely pretends to hold a position in the public service with purpose to induce another to submit to such pretended official authority or otherwise to act in reliance upon that pretense.

L.1978, c. 95, s. 2C:28-8, eff. Sept. 1, 1979.

2C:43-3. Fines and Restitutions.

A person who has been convicted of an offense may be sentenced to pay a fine, to make restitution, or both, such fine not to exceed:

***

c. $1,000.00, when the conviction is of a disorderly persons offense;

d. $500.00, when the conviction is of a petty disorderly persons offense;

e. Any higher amount equal to double the pecuniary gain to the offender or loss to the victim caused by the conduct constituting the offense by the offender. In such case the court shall make a finding as to the amount of the gain or loss, and if the record does not contain sufficient evidence to support such a finding the court may conduct a hearing upon the issue. For purposes of this section the term "gain" means the amount of money or the value of property derived by the offender and "loss" means the amount of value separated from the victim or the amount of any payment owed to the victim and avoided or evaded and includes any reasonable and necessary expense incurred by the owner in recovering or replacing lost, stolen or damaged property, or recovering any payment avoided or evaded, and, with respect to property of a research facility, includes the cost of repeating an interrupted or invalidated experiment or loss of profits. The term "victim" shall mean a person who suffers a personal, physical or psychological injury or death or incurs loss of or injury to personal or real property as a result of a crime committed against that person, or in the case of a homicide, the nearest relative of the victim. The terms "gain" and "loss" shall also mean, where appropriate, the amount of any tax, fee, penalty and interest avoided, evaded, or otherwise unpaid or improperly retained or disposed of;

f. Any higher amount specifically authorized by another section of this code or any other statute;

***

The restitution ordered paid to the victim shall not exceed the victim's loss, except that in any case involving the failure to pay any State tax, the amount of restitution to the State shall be the full amount of the tax avoided or evaded, including full civil penalties and interest as provided by law. In any case where the victim of the offense is any department or division of State government, the court shall order restitution to the victim. Any restitution imposed on a person shall be in addition to any fine which may be imposed pursuant to this section.

Amended 1979, c. 178, s. 83; 1981, c. 290, s. 37; 1987, c. 76, s. 34; 1987, c. 106, s. 10; 1991, c. 329, s. 2; 1995, c. 20, s. 6; 1995, c. 417, s. 2; 1997, c. 181, s. 12.

Title 3B. Administration of Estates — Decedents and Others

3B:3-5. Making will self-proved subsequent to time of execution

A will executed in compliance with N.J.S. 3B:3-2 may at any time subsequent to its execution be made self-proved by the acknowledgment thereof by the testator and the affidavits of the witnesses, each made before an officer authorized pursuant to R.S. 46:14-6, R.S. 46:14-7 or R.S. 46:14-8 to take acknowledgments and proofs of instruments entitled to be recorded under the laws of this State, attached or annexed to the will in substantially the following form:

The State of _____
County of _____

We, _____, _____and _____, the testator and the witnesses, respectively, whose names are signed to the attached or foregoing instrument, being duly sworn, do hereby declare to the undersigned authority that the testator signed and executed the instrument as his last will and that he had signed willingly (or willingly directed another to sign for him), and that he executed it as his free and voluntary act for the purposes therein expressed, and that each of the witnesses, in the presence and hearing of the testator, signed the will as witness and that to the best of his knowledge the testator was at that time 18 years of age or older, of sound mind and under no constraint or undue influence.

Testator _____
Witness _____
Witness _____

Subscribed, sworn to and acknowledged before me by _____, the testator, and subscribed and sworn to before me by _____and _____, witnesses, this _____ day of _____.

_____ (Signed)
_____ (Official capacity of officer)

L.1981, c. 405, s. 3B:3-5, eff. May 1, 1982.

3B:3-6. Validating acknowledgment
An acknowledgment to make a will self-proved taken on or after September 1, 1978, but before October 11, 1979, pursuant to R.S. 46:14-6, R.S. 46:14-7 or R.S. 46:14-8 to make a will self-proved under N.J.S. 3B:3-4 or N.J.S. 3B:3-5 is a valid acknowledgment, notwithstanding that the certificate of acknowledgment does not have the officer's official seal affixed thereto.
L.1981, c. 405, s. 3B:3-6, eff. May 1, 1982.

3B:3-7. Who may witness a will
Any person generally competent to be a witness may act as a witness to a will and to testify concerning the execution thereof.
L.1981, c. 405, s. 3B:3-7, eff. May 1, 1982.

3B:3-8. Will not invalidated if signed by interested witness
A will or any provision thereof is not invalid because the will is signed by an interested witness.
L.1981, c. 405, s. 3B:3-8, eff. May 1, 1982.

3B:3-9. Laws determining valid execution of will
A written will is validly executed if executed in compliance with N.J.S. 3B:3-2 or N.J.S. 3B:3-3 or its execution was in compliance with the law of the place where it was executed, or with the law of the place where at the time of execution or at the time of death the testator was domiciled, had a place of abode or was a national.
L.1981, c. 405, s. 3B:3-9, eff. May 1, 1982.

Title 7. Bills, Notes and Checks

7:5-3. Record of protest by notary
Every notary public, upon protesting any bill of exchange or promissory note, shall record in a book to be kept for that purpose the time when, place where and upon whom, demand of payment was made, with a copy of the notice of nonpayment, how and when served; or if sent, in what manner and the time when; and if sent by post, to whom the same was directed, at what place, and when the same was put into such post office, to which record he shall sign his name.

7:5-4. Certificate of protest furnished
Any notary public who shall protest any bill of exchange or

promissory note shall furnish to the person paying the costs and expenses of such protest a certificate under his hand and official seal of the matters and things required by section 7:5-3 of this title to be recorded by him.

7:5-5. Death or removal of notary; deposit of record
Upon the death or removal out of the state of such notary, the record mentioned in section 7:5-3 of this title shall be deposited in the office of the clerk of the county in which he last resided.

7:5-6. Protest of instruments held by bank or corporation by notary officer or employee thereof
Any notary public who is a stockholder, director, officer, employee or agent of a bank or other corporation may protest for nonacceptance or nonpayment bills of exchange, drafts, checks, notes and other negotiable instruments which may be owned or held for collection by such bank or other corporation, unless such notary is individually a party to such instrument.

Title 17. Corporations and Institutions for Finance and Insurance

17:14A-51. Proceedings for unpaid rental
17:14A-51. If the amount due for the rental of any vault, safe deposit box or receptacle for the storage and safekeeping of personal property of any safe deposit company or bank, savings bank, or savings and loan association authorized to conduct a safe deposit business under the laws of this State has not been paid for one year, the safe deposit company, bank, savings bank, savings and loan association may at any time after the expiration of the year send a written notice by registered mail addressed to the lessee or lessees in whose name the vault, safe deposit or receptacle stands on its records, directed to the address on its records, that if the rental for the vault, safe deposit box or receptacle is not paid within 30 days after the date of the mailing of the notice, it will have the vault, safe deposit box or receptacle opened in the presence of one of its officers and of a notary public not in its employ, and the contents thereof, if any, placed in a sealed package by the notary public, marked by him with the name of the lessee or lessees in whose name the vault, safe deposit box or receptacle stands and the estimated value thereof, and the package so sealed and marked will be placed in one of the general vaults, safes or boxes of the safe deposit company, bank, savings bank or savings and loan association. The notary's proceedings shall be set forth in a certificate under his official seal, and the certificate shall be

delivered to the savings and loan association, bank, savings bank or safe deposit company. The safe deposit company, bank, savings bank or savings and loan association shall have a lien on the contents of the vault, safe deposit box or receptacle so removed for the amount due to it for the rental of the vault, safe deposit box or receptacle up to the time of the removal of the contents, and for the costs and expenses, if any incurred in its opening, repairing and restoration for use. If the lien is not paid and discharged within one year from the opening of the vault, safe deposit box or receptacle and the removal of its contents, the safe deposit company, bank, savings bank or savings and loan association may sell the contents at public auction, or so much thereof as is required, to pay and discharge the lien and expenses of sale. A notice of the date, time and place of the sale shall be advertised in a newspaper having a general circulation in the county within which the principal office of the safe deposit company, bank, savings bank or savings and loan association is located, at least once a week for two successive weeks prior to the sale. The safe deposit company, bank, savings bank or savings and loan association may retain from the proceeds of sale the amount due to it for its lien and the expenses of sale. The balance of the proceeds of the sale and the unsold contents, if any, shall be held to be paid and delivered to the lessee or owner of the contents of the vault, safe deposit box or receptacle so sold.

If the balance of the proceeds of sale and the unsold contents, if any, remain unclaimed by the owner for the time prescribed in the "Uniform Unclaimed Property Act (1981)," R.S.46:30B-1 et seq., it shall be presumed to be abandoned and disposed of as therein provided.

Amended 1989, c. 58, s. 4.

Title 22A. Fees and Costs

22A:2-29. County clerk fees
Upon the filing, indexing, entering or recording of the following documents or papers in the office of the county clerk or deputy clerk of the Superior Court, such parties, filing or having the same recorded or indexed in the county clerk's office or with the deputy clerk of the Superior Court in the various counties in this State, shall pay the following fees in lieu of the fees heretofore provided for the filing, recording or entering of such documents or papers:***
***

Commissions and oaths--
Administering oaths to notaries public and commissioners of deeds $7.50

For issuing certificate of authority of notary to take proof, acknowledgment of[1] affidavit $3.00

For issuing each certificate of the commission and qualification of notary public for filing with other county clerks $6.00

For filing each certificate of the commission and qualification of notary public, in office of county clerk of county other than where such notary has qualified $6.00

***

L.1953, c. 22, p. 402, s. 11. Amended by L.1957, c. 224, p. 769, s. 1; L.1965, c. 123, s. 7; L.1967, c. 113, s. 1, eff. June 19, 1967; L.1980, c. 58, s. 2, eff. July 1, 1980; L.1985, c. 422, s. 4, eff. Jan. 13, 1986.

22A:4-14. Acknowledgments, proof, affidavits and oaths

For a service specified in this section, foreign commissioners of deeds, notaries public, judges and other officers authorized by law to perform such service, shall receive a fee as follows:

For administering an oath or taking an affidavit, $2.50.

For taking proof of a deed, $2.50.

For taking all acknowledgments, $2.50.

For administering oaths, taking affidavits, taking proofs of a deed, and taking acknowledgments of the grantors in the transfer of real estate, regardless of the number of such services performed in a single transaction to transfer real estate, $15.00.

For administering oaths, taking affidavits and taking acknowledgments of the mortgagors in the financing of real estate, regardless of the number of such services performed in a single transaction to finance real estate, $25.00.

Amended 1964, c. 205; 2002, c.34, s.48.

Title 26. Health and Vital Statistics

26:2H-56. Advance directive for health care; execution

4. A declarant may execute an advance directive for health care at any time. The advance directive shall be signed and dated by, or at the direction of, the declarant in the presence of two subscribing adult witnesses, who shall attest that the declarant is of sound mind and free of duress and undue influence. A designated health care representative shall not act as a witness to the execution of an advance directive. Alternatively, the advance directive shall be signed and dated by, or at the direction of, the declarant and be acknowledged by the declarant before a notary public, attorney at law, or other person authorized to administer oaths. An advance directive may be supplemented by a video or audio tape recording. A female declarant may include in an advance directive executed

---

[1]As in original. This should probably read "or."

by her, information as to what effect the advance directive shall
have if she is pregnant.

L.1991, c. 201, s. 4.

26:2H-57. Proxy, instruction directive; reaffirmed, modified, revoked

5. a. A declarant may reaffirm or modify either a proxy directive,
or an instruction directive, or both. The reaffirmation or
modification shall be made in accordance with the requirements for
execution of an advance directive pursuant to section 4 of this act.

b. A declarant may revoke an advance directive, including a
proxy directive, or an instruction directive, or both, by the
following means:

(1) Notification, orally or in writing, to the health care
representative, physician, nurse or other health care professional,
or other reliable witness, or by any other act evidencing an intent
to revoke the document; or

(2) Execution of a subsequent proxy directive or instruction
directive, or both, in accordance with section 4 of this act.

c. Designation of the declarant's spouse as health care
representative shall be revoked upon divorce or legal separation,
unless otherwise specified in the advance directive.

d. An incompetent patient may suspend an advance directive,
including a proxy directive, an instruction directive, or both, by any
of the means stated in paragraph (1) of subsection b. of this section.
An incompetent patient who has suspended an advance directive
may reinstate that advance directive by oral or written notification
to the health care representative, physician, nurse or other health
care professional of an intent to reinstate the advance directive.

e. Reaffirmation, modification, revocation or suspension of an
advance directive is effective upon communication to any person
capable of transmitting the information including the health care
representative, the attending physician, nurse or other health care
professional responsible for the patient's care.

L.1991, c. 201, s. 5.

Title 41. Oaths and Affidavits

41:1-6. Affirmations and declarations; when authorized; forms; legal effect

Every person, permitted or required to take an oath in any case,
where, by law, an oath is allowed or required, and who shall allege
that he is conscientiously scrupulous of taking an oath, shall,
instead of an oath, be permitted to make solemn affirmation or
declaration in one of the following forms, to wit:

"I, _____, do solemnly, sincerely and truly declare and affirm" : or,

"I, _____, do declare, in the presence of Almighty God, the witness of the truth of what I say"

Either of which forms shall be as good and effectual in law, as an oath taken in the usual form. In the affirmation or declaration, the words "so help me God", at the close of the usual oath, shall be omitted.

Every person empowered and required to tender and administer an oath in the usual form, is empowered and required to tender and administer the affirmation or declaration prescribed by this section, when requested so to do by any such scrupulous person.

41:1-7. Seal not necessary to validity of oath or affidavit

It shall not be necessary to the validity or sufficiency of any oath, affirmation or affidavit, made or taken before any of the persons named in section 41:2-1 of this title, that the same shall be certified under the official seal of the officer before whom made.

41:2-1. Officers authorized to take oaths

All oaths, affirmations and affidavits required to be made or taken by law of this State, or necessary or proper to be made, taken or used in any court of this State, or for any lawful purpose whatever, may be made and taken before any one of the following officers:

The Chief Justice of the Supreme Court or any of the justices or judges of courts of record of this State;

Masters of the Superior Court;

Municipal judges;

Mayors or aldermen of cities, towns or boroughs or commissioners of commission governed municipalities;

Surrogates, registers of deeds and mortgages, county clerks and their deputies;

Municipal clerks and clerks of boards of chosen freeholders;

Sheriffs of any county;

Members of boards of chosen freeholders;

Clerks of all courts;

Notaries public;

Commissioners of deeds;

Members of the State Legislature;

Attorneys-at-law and counsellors-at-law of this State.

This section shall not apply to official oaths required to be made or taken by any of the officers of this State, nor to oaths or affidavits required to be made and taken in open court.

Amended by L.1951, c. 302, p. 1084, s. 1; L.1953, c. 39, p. 752, s.

1; L.1953, c. 428, p. 2152, s. 3; L.1964, c. 165, s. 1; L.1968, c. 169, s. 1, eff. July 16, 1968; L.1970, c. 182, s. 1, eff. Aug. 19, 1970; L.1983, c. 495, s. 1, eff. Jan. 17, 1984; L.1986, c. 124, s. 1, eff. Oct. 9, 1986.

41:2-3 Oaths administered by notaries public in financial institution matters.

a. A notary public who is a stockholder, director, officer, employee or agent of a financial institution or other corporation may administer an oath to any other stockholder, director, officer, employee or agent of the corporation.

b. A notary public employed by a financial institution may follow directions or policies of the employer which provide that during the hours of the notary public's employment by the financial institution the notary public shall not administer oaths except in the course of the business of the employer.

As used in this section, "financial institution" means a State or federally chartered bank, savings bank, savings and loan association or credit union.

Amended 1997, c. 340.

41:2-14. Oaths of office of notaries, etc.

In case of the absence, removal, death, or any other disability of the county clerk of any county, any judge of the Superior Court may administer the oaths of office and allegiance to commissioners of deeds, notaries public or other persons required to take the same before such clerk, and any official's oath so administered shall be as effectual in law as if taken in the manner prescribed by law.

Amended 1953, c. 39, s. 10; 1991, c. 91, s. 407.

41:2-17. Officers authorized to administer or take; jurat; certificate

Any oath, affirmation or affidavit required or authorized to be taken in any suit or legal proceeding in this state, or for any lawful purpose whatever, except official oaths and depositions required to be taken upon notice, when taken out of this state, may be taken before any notary public of the state, territory, nation, kingdom or country in which the same shall be taken, or before any officer who may be authorized by the laws of this state to take the acknowledgment of deeds in such state, territory, nation, kingdom or country; and a recital that he is such notary or officer in the jurat or certificate of such oath, affirmation or affidavit, and his official designation annexed to his signature, and attested under his official seal, shall be sufficient proof that the person before whom the same is taken is such notary or officer. When, however, any other certificate is required by law to be annexed to the certificate of such officer, other than a notary public, for the recording of a deed acknowledged before him, a like certificate shall be annexed to his certificate of the taking of such oath.

Title 46. Property

46:14-2.1. Acknowledgment and proof.

a. To acknowledge a deed or other instrument the maker of the instrument shall appear before an officer specified in R.S.46:14-6.1 and acknowledge that it was executed as the maker's own act. To acknowledge a deed or other instrument made on behalf of a corporation or other entity, the maker shall appear before an officer specified in R.S.46:14-6.1 and state that the maker was authorized to execute the instrument on behalf of the entity and that the maker executed the instrument as the act of the entity.

b. To prove a deed or other instrument, a subscribing witness shall appear before an officer specified in R.S.46:14-6.1 and swear that he or she witnessed the maker of the instrument execute the instrument as the maker's own act. To prove a deed or other instrument executed on behalf of a corporation or other entity, a subscribing witness shall appear before an officer specified in R.S.46:14-6.1 and swear that the representative was authorized to execute the instrument on behalf of the entity, and that he or she witnessed the representative execute the instrument as the act of the entity.

c. The officer taking an acknowledgment or proof shall sign a certificate stating that acknowledgment or proof. The certificate shall also state:

(1) that the maker or the witness personally appeared before the officer;

(2) that the officer was satisfied that the person who made the acknowledgment or proof was the maker of or the witness to the instrument;

(3) the jurisdiction in which the acknowledgment or proof was taken;

(4) the officer's name and title;

(5) the date on which the acknowledgment was taken.

d. The seal of the officer taking the acknowledgment or proof need not be affixed to the certificate stating that acknowledgment or proof.

L.1991, c. 308, s. 1.

46:14-4.1. Proof of instruments not acknowledged or proved.

If a deed or other instrument cannot be acknowledged or proved for any reason, the instrument may be proved in Superior Court by proof of handwriting or otherwise to the satisfaction of the court. Notice of the application in accordance with the Rules of Court shall be given to any party whose interests may be affected.

L.1991, c. 308, s. 1.

46:14-4.2. Signatures.

For purposes of this title, a signature includes any mark made on a document by a person who thereby intends to give legal effect to the document. A signature also includes any mark made on a document on behalf of a person, with that person's authority and to effectuate that person's intent.

L.1991, c. 308, s. 1.

46:14-6.1. Officers authorized to take acknowledgments.

a. The officers of this State authorized to take acknowledgments or proofs in this State, or in any other United States or foreign jurisdiction, are:

(1) an attorney-at-law;

(2) a notary public;

(3) a county clerk or deputy county clerk;

(4) a register of deeds and mortgages or a deputy register;

(5) a surrogate or deputy surrogate.

b. The officers authorized to take acknowledgments or proofs, in addition to those listed in subsection a., are:

(1) any officer of the United States, of a state, territory or district of the United States, or of a foreign nation authorized at the time and place of the acknowledgment or proof by the laws of that jurisdiction to take acknowledgments or proofs. If the certificate of acknowledgment or proof does not designate the officer as a justice, judge or notary, the certificate of acknowledgment or proof, or an affidavit appended to it, shall contain a statement of the officer's authority to take acknowledgments or proofs;

(2) a foreign commissioner of deeds for New Jersey within the jurisdiction of the commission;

(3) a foreign service or consular officer or other representative of the United States to any foreign nation, within the territory of that nation.

L.1991, c. 308, s. 1.

46:14-8. Officers without United States before whom deeds or instruments may be acknowledged or proved; methods; certificates; proof of authority

If the party who shall have executed or who shall execute any deed or instrument of the description or nature set forth in section 46:16-1 of this Title, or the witnesses thereto, shall have happened or shall happen to be in any foreign kingdom, State, nation or colony, whether resident in this State, or in such foreign kingdom, State, nation or colony, or elsewhere, an acknowledgment or proof such as is prescribed by section 46:14-6 of this Title, made before and certified by any one of the officers herein named, shall be as good and effectual as if the same had been made within this State before an officer authorized to take acknowledgments or proofs within the State and had been certified by him, as provided in section 46:14-6.

The officers authorized to take acknowledgments or proofs under authority of this section are:

(a) Any master of the Superior Court or attorney-at-law of New Jersey;

(b) Any public ambassador, minister, consul, vice-consul, consular agent, charge d'affaires or other representative of the United States for the time being, to or at any such foreign kingdom, State, nation or colony;

(c) Any court of law of such foreign kingdom, State, nation or colony;

(d) Any notary, notary public, commissioner for oaths, mayor or other chief magistrate, of and then having been or being within any city, borough, or corporation of such foreign kingdom, State, nation or colony, in which city, borough or corporation such party or witnesses may have happened or may happen to be.

Acknowledgments or proofs taken or made by a court of law, a notary, notary public, commissioner for oaths, or a mayor or other chief magistrate under authority of this section shall be certified if taken by said court under the official seal of said court, and the hand of the judge or clerk thereof, or under the official seal, if any, and the hand of any other person hereby authorized to take acknowledgments or proofs; and such certificate of acknowledgment or proof shall be sufficient proof as to the existence and authority of said court, mayor, notary or other officer.

Amended by L.1939, c. 166, p. 516, s. 1, eff. July 11, 1939; L.1949, c. 279, p. 870, s. 3; L.1963, c. 81, s. 12, eff. June 4, 1963.

46:15-1.1. Prerequisites to recordation.

a. Any instrument affecting title to or interest in real estate or containing any agreement in relation to real estate in this State shall be recorded on presentation to the recording officer of any county in which all or part of the real estate is located, if it appears that:

(1) the instrument is in English or accompanied by a translation into English;

(2) the instrument bears a signature;

(3) the instrument is acknowledged or proved in the manner provided by this title;

(4) the names appear typed, printed or stamped beneath the signatures of any parties to the instrument and the officer before whom it was acknowledged or proved;

(5) any required recordation fee is paid; and

(6) if the instrument is a deed conveying real property, (a) it fulfills the requirements of P.L.1968, c.49, s.2 (C.46:15-6), (b) it includes the name and signature of its preparer on its first page and (c) it includes a reference to the lot and block number of the property conveyed as designated on the tax map of the municipality at the time of the conveyance or the account number

of the property. If the property has been subdivided, the reference shall be preceded by the words "part of." If no lot and block or account number has been assigned to the property, the deed shall state that fact.

b. An instrument, to be entitled to recordation, whether made by an individual or by a corporation or other entity, is not required to be executed under seal, or to contain words referring to execution under seal.

L.1991, c. 308, s. 2.

Title 52. State Government, Departments and Officers

52:6-12. Appointment; number; designation and description; application; fees

a. The Secretary of State may appoint such number of commissioners resident in each of the States and territories of the United States and the District of Columbia as he may deem expedient, except where the appointments are incompatible with the laws of the jurisdiction wherein the commissioners reside. Persons thus appointed shall be commissioned by the Governor.

b. Each commissioner so appointed shall be designated a "foreign commissioner of deeds for New Jersey," and may be so described in his appointment and commission or as a "commissioner for taking the acknowledgment or proof of deeds for New Jersey in (such State, territory or district)." He may use either of these designations in his certificates.

c. A person desiring to be appointed and commissioned a foreign commissioner of deeds shall make application to the Secretary of State on a form prescribed by him and endorsed by a member of the Legislature or the Secretary of State or the Assistant Secretary of State. Renewals shall be made in the same manner as the original application. The fees required to be paid for the issuance of any commission to a person appointed as foreign commissioner of deeds for New Jersey shall be paid to the Secretary of State, who shall account to the State Treasurer for the same.

Amended by L.1947, c. 264, p. 966, s. 1; L.1981, c. 395, s. 1, eff. Jan. 6, 1982.

52:6-13. Terms of office; removal by governor

Commissioners appointed by virtue of section 52:6-12 of this title shall hold office for a term of three years. They may be removed from office at the pleasure of the governor, and shall be removed if it is made to appear to the governor that they have been or are charging more or greater fees than are allowed by law.

52:6-14. Removal from residence as vacating appointment

Except as provided in section 52:6-15 of this title, if a foreign commissioner removes out of the state, territory or district in which he resides at the time of his appointment, his commission shall thereupon be void.

52:6-15. Foreign commissioner of deeds for adjoining states

No person shall be denied appointment as a foreign commissioner of deeds of an adjoining state on account of residence outside of that State, provided such person resides in this State. The official acts of such a commissioner resident in this State and performed in an adjoining state shall be as valid and effectual as if he had resided in the adjoining state.

Amended by L.1981, c. 395, s. 2, eff. Jan. 6, 1982.

52:6-16. Fee to accompany application for commission

Each applicant for a commission as a foreign commissioner of deeds for New Jersey shall inclose with his application the fee required by section 22:4-1 of the title Fees and Costs, which shall be returned if a commission is not issued to him.

52:6-17. Official oath; by whom administered

Each foreign commissioner of deeds shall, before he enters upon the duties of his office, take and subscribe an oath to perform well and faithfully the duties of his office in accordance with the laws of this State. The oath may be administered by any person authorized to do so under R.S. 41:2-1 or R.S. 41:2-17.

Amended by L.1981, c. 395, s. 3, eff. Jan. 6, 1982.

52:6-18. Seal; impression of filed with secretary of state

Each foreign commissioner of deeds shall attest his official acts by an official seal, an impression of which, in wax or other appropriate substance shall, with his official oath, be filed in the office of the secretary of state of this state.

52:6-20. Use and effect of official certificates

The official certificates of a foreign commissioner of deeds attested by his official seal may be indorsed upon or annexed to any instrument of writing for use or record in this state, and shall be entitled to full faith and credit.

52:6-21. Manual; provision to applicants

The secretary of state shall provide to each applicant a manual prescribing the powers and duties of a foreign commissioner of deeds.

Amended by L.1981, c. 395, s. 4, eff. Jan. 6, 1982.

52:6-22. List of foreign commissioners of deeds
The secretary of state shall maintain a list of all foreign commissioners of deeds including the dates of their appointment and the expiration of their terms.

Amended by L.1981, c. 395, s. 5, eff. Jan. 6, 1982.

New Jersey Rules of Civil Practice

Rule 4:12. Persons before whom depositions may be taken; authority

4:12-1. Within the state
Within the State, depositions shall be taken before a person authorized by the laws of this State to administer oaths.

4:12-2. Without the state but within the United States
Outside this State but within the United States or within a territory or insular possession subject to the dominion of the United States, depositions may be taken before a person authorized to administer oaths by the laws of this State, of the United States or of the place where the examination is held.

4:12-3. In foreign countries
In a foreign country depositions shall be taken (a) on notice before a secretary of embassy or legation, consul general, consul, vice consul, or consular agent of the United States, or (b) before such person or officer as may be appointed by commission or under letters rogatory. A commission or letters rogatory shall be issued only when necessary or convenient, on application and notice, and on such terms and with such directions as are appropriate. Officers may be designated in notices or commissions either by name or descriptive title and letters rogatory may be addresses. "To the Appropriate Judicial Authority in (here name the country)."

4:12-4. Disqualification for interest
No deposition shall be taken before or by a person who is a relative, employee or attorney of a party or relative or employee of such attorney or is financially interested in an action.

New Jersey Rules of Criminal Practice

Rule 3:13-2. Depositions
(a) When and how taken. If it appears to the judge of the court in which the indictment or accusation is pending that a material witness may be unable to attend or may be prevented from attending the trial of the indictment or accusation, or any hearing

in connection therewith, the court, prevent injustice, may upon motion and notice to the parties order that the testimony of such witnesses be taken, orally by deposition as provided in civil actions and that any designated books, papers, documents or tangible objects, not privileged, be produced at the same time and place. If a witness is committed for failure to give bail to appear to testify at a trial or hearing, the court on written motion of the witness and upon notice to the parties may direct that his deposition be taken, and after the deposition has been subscribed the court may discharge the witness. The transcript of all depositions shall be filed with the county clerk as provided in civil actions.

(b) Use. [Omitted.]

(c) Objections to admissibility. Objections to receiving a deposition or part thereof in evidence may be made as provided in civil actions. ■

State Offices Governing Notaries

For walk-in or courier service:
State of New Jersey
Notary Public Section
225 W. State Street
Trenton, NJ 08608-1001
Telephone: (609) 292-9292

For mail service:
New Jersey Department of Treasury
Division of Revenue
Notary Public Section
P.O. Box 452
Trenton, NJ 08625
Telephone: (609) 292-9292

For general online information, visit the official Website of the State of New Jersey at *http://www.state.nj.us.* For information regarding Notaries Public, go to the home page for the Notary Public Section and the Division of Commercial Recording at *http://www.state.nj.us/treasury /revenue/dcr/programs/notary.html.* ■

County Clerks' Offices

Within three months of receiving a Notary commission, each Notary must take an oath of office from the county clerk of the county in which he or she resides. For nonresidents, the oath must be filed in the county in which the applicant maintains a place of employment.

At these same offices, certificates authenticating a local Notary's signature on documents may be obtained by anyone presenting the document notarized by the particular local Notary.

For certified copies of marriage certificates, contact the office of the county clerk in which the marriage certificate was filed.

Atlantic County
5901 Main Street
CN 2005
Mays Landing, NJ 08330
(609) 645-5839

Bergen County
One Bergen County Plaza
Hackensack, NJ 07601
(201) 336-7000

Burlington County
Court Complex
P.O. Box 6000
49 Rancocas Road
Mount Holly, NJ 08060
(609) 265-5188

Camden County
Camden County Courthouse,
Rm. 102
520 Market Street
Camden, NJ 08102
(865) 225-5300

Cape May County
7 North Main Street
P.O. Box 5000
Cape May, NJ 08210-5000
(609) 465-1010

Cumberland County
Court House60 West Broad Street
Bridgeton, NJ 08302-2665
(856) 451-8000, ext. 4864

Essex County
465 King Blvd., Room 245
Newark, NJ 07102
(973) 621-4921

Gloucester County
Courthouse, 1st Floor
P.O. Box 129
Woodbury, NJ 08096-3327
(856) 853-3237

Hudson County
583 Newark Avenue
Jersey City, NJ 07306-2018
(201) 795-6112

Hunterdon County
71 Main Street
Hall of Records
Flemington, NJ 08822-2900
(908) 788-1221

Mercer County
Courthouse
209 S. Broad Street
Trenton, NJ 08650-8068
(609) 989-6467

Middlesex County
County Administration Building
John F. Kennedy Square,
P.O. Box 1110
New Brunswick, NJ 08901
(732) 745-3870

Monmouth County
Market Yard
P.O. Box 1251
Freehold, NJ 07728
(732) 431-7324

Morris County
P.O. Box 315 — Court St.
Hall of Record,
Administration Building.
Morristown, NJ 07963-0315
(973) 285-6060

Ocean County
P.O. Box 2191
Courthouse, Room 103
Toms River, NJ 08754-2191
(732) 929-2032

Passaic County
401 Grand Street, Room 130
Paterson, NJ 07505
(973) 225-3632

Salem County
92 Market Street
P.O. Box 18
Salem, NJ 08079-1913
(856) 935-7510

Somerset County
P.O. Box 3000
20 Grove Street
Administration Building
Somerville, NJ 08876-1262
(908) 231-7006

Sussex County
4 Park Place
Hall of Records
Newton, NJ 07860
(973) 579-0900

Union County
Courthouse
2 Broad Street
Elizabeth, NJ 07207
(908) 527-4966

Warren County
413 Second St.
Courthouse
Belvidere, NJ 07823-1500
(908) 475-6211

Bureaus of Vital Statistics

New Jersey Notaries are not authorized to certify copies of public records. Persons requesting "notarization," "certification," or certified copies of birth or death certificates should be referred to the appropriate state public office, below, that can provide certified copies of vital records.

Persons requiring copies of foreign records should contact the appropriate consulate in the United States.

Alabama
Vital Records
Department of Public Health
P.O. Box 5625
Montgomery, AL 36103-5625

Alaska
Bureau of Vital Statistics
Dept. of Health & Social Services
5441 Commercial Bl.
Juneau, AK 99801

Arizona
Office of Vital Records
Dept. of Health Services
P.O. Box 3887
Phoenix, AZ 85030-3887

Arkansas
Division of Vital Records
Department of Health
4815 West Markham Street, Slot 44
Little Rock, AR 72205-3867

California
Office of Vital Records
Department of Health Services
P.O. Box 997410, MS: 5103
Sacramento, CA 95899-7410

Colorado
Health Statistics
Department of Health
CHEIS-HS-A1
4300 Cherry Creek Drive South
Denver, CO 80246-1530

Connecticut
(Certified copies are not available from the state office. Requests must be made to the place where the event occurred.)

Delaware
Office of Vital Statistics
Division of Public Health
P.O. Box 637
Dover, DE 19903

District of Columbia
Department of Health
John A. Wilson Building
1350 Pennsylvania Avenue
NW
Washington, DC 20004

Florida
Department of Health
Office of Vital Statistics
4052 Bald Cypress
WayTallahassee, FL 32399-
1701

Georgia
Vital Records
2600 Skyland Drive NE
Atlanta, GA 30319-3640

Hawaii
State Department of Health
Vital Statistics Section
P.O. Box 3378
Honolulu, HI 96801

Idaho
Department of Health and
Welfare
Vital Statistics Unit
450 West State Street, 1st
Floor
P.O. Box 83720
Boise, ID 83720

Illinois
Health Statistics
Department of Public
Health
605 West Jefferson Street
Springfield, IL 62702-5097

Indiana
Vital Records Section
State Department of Health
2 North Meridian Street
Indianapolis, IN 46204

Iowa
Department of Public
Health
Bureau of Vital Records
Lucas Office Building, 1st
Floor
321 East 12th Street
Des Moines, IA 50319-0075

Kansas
Office of Vital Statistics
1000 SW Jackson Street,
Suite 120
Topeka, KS 66612

Kentucky
Office of Vital Statistics
Department for Health
Services
275 East Main Street-IE-A
Frankfort, KY 40621-0001

Louisiana
Vital Records Registry
Office of Public Health
325 Loyola Avenue
P.O. Box 60630
New Orleans, LA 70160

Maine
Department of Human
Services
Vital Records
221 State Street, Station 11
11 State House Station
Augusta, ME 04333-0011

Maryland
Division of Vital Records
6550 Reisterstown Plaza
Reiserstown Road Plaza
Baltimore, MD 21215

Massachusetts
Vital Records and Statistics
150 Mt. Vernon Street, First
Floor
Dorchester, MA 02125-3105

Michigan
Department of Community
Health
3423 N. Martin Luther King
Blvd.
P. O. Box 30721
Lansing, MI 48909

Minnesota
Department of Health
Attn: Office of the State
Registrar
717 Delaware Street, SE
P.O. Box 9441
Minneapolis, MN 55440-
9441

Mississippi
Vital Records
571 Stadium Drive
P.O. Box 1700
Jackson, MS 39215-1700

Missouri
Department of Health
Bureau of Vital Records
930 Wildwood
P.O. Box 570
Jefferson City, MO 65102

Montana
Office of Vital Statistics
Department of Public
Health
P.O. Box 4210
111 North Sanders, Room
209
Helena, MT 59604

Nebraska
Vital Statistics
Department of Health
P.O. Box 95044
Lincoln, NE 68509-5044

Nevada
Division of Health / Vital
Statistics
505 East King Street, Room
#102
Carson City, NV 89701

New Hampshire
Bureau of Vital Records
29 Hazen Drive
Concord, NH 03301

New Jersey
Vital Statistics
Customer Service Unit
P.O. Box 370
Trenton, NJ 08625-0370

New Mexico
Vital Records and Health
Statistics
P.O. Box 26110
1105 St. Francis Drive
Santa Fe, NM 87502

New York
Certification Unit
Vital Records Section
800 North Pearl Street, 2nd
Floor
Menands, NY 12204

New York City
Office of Vital Records
NYC Department of Health
and Mental Hygiene
125 Worth Street, CN4,
Room 133
New York, NY 10013-4090

North Carolina
Vital Records
1903 Mail Service Center
Raleigh, NC 27699-1903

North Dakota
Division of Vital Records
600 East Boulevard Ave.
Department 301
Bismarck, ND 58505-0200

Ohio
Vital Statistics
246 North High Street
1st Floor
Columbus, OH 43216

Oklahoma
Vital Records Service
State Department of Health
1000 Northeast Tenth,
Room 111
Oklahoma City, OK 73117

Oregon
Oregon Vital Records
800 NE Oregon Street, Ste
205
PO Box 14050
Portland, OR 97293

Pennsylvania
Vital Records
State Department of Health
101 S. Mercer Street
P.O. Box 1528
New Castle, PA 16101

Rhode Island
Office of Vital Records
Department of Health
3 Capitol Hill
Room 101
Providence, RI 02908-5097

South Carolina
Office of Vital Records
2600 Bull Street
Columbia, SC 29201

South Dakota
Department of Health
Vital Records
600 East Capitol Avenue
Pierre, SD 57501-2536

Tennessee
Vital Records
Central Services Building
1st Floor
421 5th Avenue North
Nashville, TN 37247

Texas
Bureau of Vital Statistics
Department of Health
P.O. Box 12040
Austin, TX 78711-2040

Utah
Vital Records & Statistics
Cannon Health Building
288 North 1460 West
P.O. Box 141012
Salt Lake City, UT 84114-1012

Vermont
Department of Health
Vital Records Section
108 Cherry Street
P.O. Box 70
Burlington, VT 05402-0070

Virginia
Office of Vital Records
P.O. Box 1000
Richmond, VA 23218

Washington
Department of Health
Center for Health Statistics
P.O. Box 9709
Olympia, WA 98507-9709

West Virginia
Vital Registration Office
350 Capitol Street,
Room 165
Charleston, WV 25301-3701

Wisconsin
Vital Records
1 West Wilson Street
P.O. Box 309
Madison, WI 53701-0309

Wyoming
Vital Records Services
Hathaway Building
Cheyenne, WY 82002

American Samoa
Registrar of Vital Statistics
Vital Statistics Section
Government of American
Samoa
Pago Pago, AS 96799

Guam
Department of Public
Health and Social Services
Government of Guam
P.O. Box 2816
Agana, GU M.I. 96932

Northern Mariana Islands
Commonwealth Recorder
Superior Court
Vital Records Section
P.O. Box 500307
Saipan, MP 96910

Panama Canal Zone
Vital Records Section
Passport Services
U.S. Department of State
1111 19th Street NW, Suite
510
Washington, DC, CZ 34011-
2300

Puerto Rico
Department of Health
Demographic Registry
P.O. Box 11854
Fernández Juncos Station
San Juan, PR 00910

Virgin Islands (St. Croix)
Department of Health
Vital Statistics
Charles Harwood
Memorial Complex
Christiansted, St. Croix, VI
00820

**Virgin Islands (St.
Thomas,
St. John)**
Department of Health
Vital Statistics
Old Municipal Hospital
St. Thomas, VI 00802 ■

Hague Convention Nations

The nations listed on the following pages are parties to a treaty called the Hague Convention Abolishing the Requirement of Legalization (Authentication) for Foreign Public Documents.

Treaty Simplifies Authentication. A Notary's signature on documents that are sent to these nations may be authenticated (verified as valid for the benefit of the recipient in the foreign nation) through attachment of a single certificate of capacity called an *apostille*. The *apostille* (French for "notation") is the only authentication certificate necessary. Nations not subscribing to the Hague Convention may require as many as five or six separate authenticating certificates from different governmental agencies, domestic and foreign.

How to Request an *Apostille*. To obtain an *apostille*, mail the notarized document, a self-addressed stamped envelope and a $25 check - or $5 per certificate if the document relates to adoption of a child - payable to the "Treasurer, State of New Jersey" to:

Address:
Department of Treasury
Division of Revenue
Notary Public Unit
P.O. Box 452,
Trenton, NJ 08625
Telephone: (609) 292-9292

In Person, Go to:
State of New Jersey
Notary Public Section
225 West State Street
Trenton, NJ 08608-1001

An *apostille* must be specifically requested, indicating the nation to which the document will be sent. It is *not* the Notary's responsibility to obtain an *apostille*, but rather, it is the responsibility of the party sending the document.

Hague Convention Nations. The following nations participate in the Hague Convention:

Albania	Estonia
Andorra[10]	Fiji[10]
Antigua and Barbuda[10]	Finland
Argentina[1]	France[3]
Armenia[10]	Germany
Australia	Greece
Austria	Grenada[10]
Azerbaijan	Honduras[10]
Bahamas[10]	Hong Kong[4]
Barbados[10]	Hungary
Belarus	Iceland
Belgium	Ireland
Belize[10]	Israel
Bosnia-Herzegovina[2]	Italy
Botswana[10]	Japan
Brunei Darussalam[10]	Kazakhstan[10]
Bulgaria	Latvia
Colombia[10]	Lesotho[10]
Cook Islands	Liberia[5]
Croatia[2]	Liechtenstein[10]
Cyprus	Lithuania
Czech Republic	Luxembourg
Dominica[10]	Macao[4]
Ecuador	Macedonia[2]
El Salvador[10]	Malawi[10]

1. Excludes recognition of extension of the Convention by the United Kingdom to the Malvinas (Falkland Islands), South Georgia, South Sandwich Islands and the Argentine Antarctic Sector.

2. The former Yugoslavia was a party to the Convention. Only the breakaway nations of Bosnia-Herzegovina, Croatia, Macedonia, Serbia and Montenegro, and Slovenia have confirmed that the Convention still applies.

3. Including *Comoros Islands*, *Djibouti*, French Guyana, French Polynesia, Guadeloupe, Martinique, New Caledonia, Reunion, St. Pierre and Miquelon, and Wallis and Futuna. (Names appearing in regular type denote territories; *italic type denotes now-independent nations that have not affirmed participation in the Convention.*)

4. Retained status as Hague nation after control was returned to China on July 1, 1997 (Hong Kong) and December 20, 1999 (Macao).

5. Convention does not apply between Liberia and the U.S. Liberia is a nonmember of the Convention which is a contracting state or has signed to the Convention.

10. Nonmember of the Convention which is a contracting state or has signed to the Convention.

Mauritius[10]

Mexico

Monaco

Namibia[10]

Netherlands[6]

New Zealand

Niue[10]

Norway

Panama

Portugal[7]

Romania

Russian Federation

Saint Kitts and Nevis[10]

Saint Lucia[10]

Saint Vincent and
  the Grenadines[10]

Samoa[10]

San Marino[10]

Serbia and Montenegro[2]

Seychelles[10]

Slovakia

Slovenia[2]

South Africa

Spain

Suriname

Swaziland[10]

Sweden

Switzerland

Tonga[10]

Trinidad and Tobago[10]

Turkey

Ukraine

United Kingdom[8]

United States[9]

Venezuela

Inquiries. Persons having questions about the Hague Convention Abolishing the Requirement of Legalization for Foreign Public Documents may address their inquiries to:

> Authentication Office
> 518 23rd Street, N.W.
> State Annex 1
> Washington, DC 20037
> (202) 647-5002

2. The former Yugoslavia was a party to the Convention. Only the breakaway nations of Bosnia-Herzegovina, Croatia, Macedonia, Serbia and Montenegro, and Slovenia have confirmed that the Convention still applies.

6. Extended to all Aruba, Curacao, and Netherlands Antilles.

7. Extended to Angola, Mozambique, and all overseas territories.

8. United Kingdom of Great Britain and Northern Ireland is extended to Anguilla, Bermuda, British Antarctica Territory, British Virgin Islands, Cayman Islands, Falkland Islands, Gibraltar, Guyana, Guernsey, Isle of Man Jersey, *Kiribati,* Montserrat, St. Helena, Solomon Islands, Turks and Caicos Islands, *Tuvalu, Vanuatu,* and *Zimbabwe.* (Names appearing in regular type denote territories; *italic type denotes now-independent nations that have not affirmed participation in the Convention.*)

9. Includes American Samoa, District of Columbia, Guam, Northern Mariana Islands, Puerto Rico, and U.S. Virgin Islands.

10. Nonmember of the Convention which is a contracting state or has signed to the Convention. ∎

About
the NNA

Since 1957, the nonprofit National Notary Association — a nonprofit educational organization — has served the nation's Notaries Public with a wide variety of instructional programs and services.

As the country's clearinghouse for information on notarial laws, customs and practices, the NNA educates Notaries through publications, seminars, annual conferences and a Notary Information Service that offers immediate answers to specific questions about notarization.

Association is perhaps most widely known as the preeminent source of information for and about Notaries. NNA works include:

- *The National Notary*, a magazine for National Notary Association members featuring how-to articles and practical tips on notarizing.

- *Notary Bulletin,* an eNewsletter that keeps NNA members up to date on developments affecting Notaries, especially new state laws and regulations.

- *Notary Basics Made Easy*, a first-of-its-kind video instruction program that simplifies Notary practices and procedures.

- *Notary Home Study Course*, a work-at-your-own-speed course covering every facet of notarization.

- *Sorry, No Can Do!* series, four volumes that help Notaries explain to customers and bosses why some requests for notarizations are improper and cannot be accommodated.

- *U.S. Notary Reference Manual*, invaluable for any person relying upon the authenticity and correctness of legal documents.

- *Notary Public Practices & Glossary*, widely hailed as the Notary's bible, a definitive reference book on notarial procedures.

- State *Notary Law Primers*, explaining a state's notarial statutes in easy-to-understand language.

- *The Model Notary Act*, prototype legislation conceived in 1973 and updated in 1984, 2002 and 2010 by an NNA-recruited panel of secretaries of state, legislators and attorneys, and regularly used by state legislatures in revising their Notary laws.

- *Notary Law & Practice: Cases & Materials*, the definitive and one-of-a-kind text for teaching Notary law to law students in schools and to attorneys in Minimum Continuing Education Seminars (MCLE), discussing every major judicial decision affecting the Notary's duties.

- *Notary Signing Agent Certification Course*, invaluable for candidates preparing to complete the Notary Signing Agent Certification Examination developed by the National Notary Association.

- Public-service pamphlets informing the general public about the function of a Notary, including *What Is A Notary Public?*, printed in English and Spanish.

In addition, the National Notary Association offers the highest quality professional supplies, including official seals and stamps, embossers, recordkeeping journals, affidavit stamps, thumbprinting devices and notarial certificates.

Though dedicated primarily to educating and assisting Notaries, the National Notary Association devotes part of its resources to helping lawmakers draft effective notarial statutes and to informing the public about the Notary's vital role in modern society. ■

Index

Page numbers listed in **bold** indicate where the most complete information on a subject can be found. *Italics* indicate the pages where the statutes pertaining to a subject are located.

Page numbers listed in **bold** indicate where the most complete information on a subject can be found. *Italics* indicate the pages where the statutes pertaining to a subject are located.

M

Page numbers listed in **bold** indicate where the most complete information on a subject can be found. *Italics* indicate the pages where the statutes pertaining to a subject are located.

N

Page numbers listed in **bold** indicate where the most complete information on a subject can be found. *Italics* indicate the pages where the statutes pertaining to a subject are located.

Page numbers listed in **bold** indicate where the most complete information on a subject can be found. *Italics* indicate the pages where the statutes pertaining to a subject are located.